IDEAS ON TRIAL

SALLY RIDE

SPACE PIONEER

Lorraine Jean Hopping

McGraw-Hill

New York St. Louis San Francisco Auckland Bogotá Caracas
Lisbon London Madrid Mexico City Milan Montreal
New Delhi San Juan Singapore Sydney Tokyo Toronto

A Bank Street Biography

To Irene, Sophia, and Daniel,
the Mars generation

Ideas on Trial

The *Ideas on Trial* series presents dramatic stories of men and women in science and medicine who waged heroic struggles and risked their comfort, freedom, reputations, and sometimes their lives, for the sake of pursuing their work.

The authors use a docu-drama, "you are there" style to tell these exciting stories. Wherever possible, actual reported scenes and dialog are used, along with quotes from letters, diaries, newspapers, and journals of the time. In a few cases, however, the authors had to invent scenes and dialog for events that did occur, but for which there was no reported scene or dialog.

Library of Congress Cataloging-in-Publication Data
Hopping, Lorraine Jean.
    Sally Ride : space pioneer / Lorraine Jean Hopping.
        p. cm.
    At head of title: Ideas on trial.
    Summary: A biography of the first woman in space, discussing her childhood, career as an astronaut, and place in history.
        ISBN 0-07-135740-8
        1. Ride, Sally—Juvenile literature. 2. Women astronauts—United States—Biography—Juvenile literature. [1. Ride, Sally. 2. Astronauts. 3. Women—Biography.] I. Title.

TL789.85.R53 H67 2000
629.45'0092—dc21
[B]   99-086768

1 2 3 4 5 6 7 8 9 0   DOC/DOC   0 9 8 7 6 5 4 3 2 1 0

ISBN 0-07-135740-8

The Bank Street Series Project Editor was Elisabeth Jakab and the Developmental Editor was Mary Loebig Giles.

The sponsoring editor for this book was Griffin Hansbury, the editing supervisor was Janice Race, and the production supervisor was Charles H. Annis. The cover and text were designed and set in New Century Schoolbook by Marsha Cohen/ Parallelogram Graphics.

McGraw-Hill books are available at special quantity discounts to use as premiums and sales promotions, or for use in corporate training programs. For more information, please write to the Director of Special Sales, McGraw-Hill, Two Penn Plaza, New York, NY, 10121-2298.

DATE DUE

SALLY RIDE
SPACE PIONEER

Dr. Sally K. Ride at Ellington Air Force Base, Texas, 1982. (NASA.)

CHILDREN'S ROOM

CONTENTS

The launch of STS-7, June 18, 1983. (NASA.)

1

SPACE IS A DANGEROUS PLACE

Lift-off was perfect.

"Too perfect," thought Sally Ride. She scanned her space shuttle instruments, looking for trouble. Nothing. Not a switch, number, needle, or dial was out of place. No warning lights flashed. No alarms sounded.

"All systems go," thought Sally. She smiled. Now she was even *thinking* in astronaut-speak. Just a year ago, before becoming an astronaut, she would have thought, "Everything looks cool."

Next, Sally focused her blue eyes on the cockpit ceiling. All eight panels of instruments were clear.

"Not for long," she thought. "There *has* to be a glitch soon. There always is."

To Sally's right, a tall Texan named John Fabian studied still more instruments. Together, John and Sally were to conduct experiments in space and test the shuttle's robotic arm. For the moment, though, they were both lookouts.

They helped the pilots watch nearly two thousand controls for signs of trouble.

Robert "Crip" Crippen, the commander of the mission, sat in front of Sally. He was one of NASA's best pilots. To Crip's right was Rick Hauck, a big, sandy-haired pilot with a bushy mustache.

"OMS two, cut-off," Crip said, flipping a switch on an overhead panel. Like most space terms, OMS, or Orbital

The Flight STS-7 Crew

Left to right, Norman E. Thagard (mission specialist), Robert L. Crippen (commander), Frederick H. Hauck (pilot), Sally K. Ride (mission specialist), and John M. Fabian (mission specialist). (NASA.)

Maneuvering System, had a simple translation: engine. It was the last engine to fire during the lift-off phase.

"Control, we have achieved orbit. Over," Crip said into a microphone.

"Roger, *Challenger*," confirmed a friendly voice from ground control. "You're looking good. Out."

"Looking too good," Sally couldn't help thinking as she glanced at the Mission Time Clock. Forty-four minutes and twenty-three seconds since lift-off and still no bumps in the road. She was almost itching for an alarm buzz or warning light. Her eyes moved from gauge to gauge. Altitude 282 kilometers... Speed Mach 20...

"Twenty times faster than the speed of sound," Sally thought. "Only astronauts get to travel *that* fast!"

Once in orbit, the lookouts, John and Sally, could relax. Sally rolled her head in a big circle to loosen her neck muscles. Then she peered out the front windows at a black field sprinkled with stars. Just beyond those windows, she tried to imagine the coldest cold possible—absolute zero. Space was just a few degrees "warmer" than that. Of course, temperature wasn't the scariest part about space. The lack of air was. The cramped cockpit formed an airtight bubble. If anything burst that bubble, a crew would die in seconds.

Bzzz! An alarm sounded.

Sally's eyes darted to a warning light. "Electrical fire in avionics bay two," she reported.

The astronauts quickly donned their portable oxygen systems, or air masks.

Sally flipped a switch marked "Av Bay 2." She lifted the

flap next to the switch, exposing a button. Then she pressed the button for a full minute to turn on the fire extinguisher in avionics bay two. Problem solved.

But then a light flashed on another panel.

"Oxygen life-support malf," Sally reported. "Malfs," or malfunctions, were serious problems. They could kill a mission—or a even a shuttle full of astronauts.

"Switching to emergency supply," Sally said. She knew the backup oxygen would last only a few hours. The crew had to find and fix the problem or abort the mission.

Bzzz! Another alarm!

"We've lost fuel cell two," Crip announced. Fuel cells create both electricity and water out of hydrogen and oxygen.

Sally looked at the power gauge and whistled. "Look at those amps falling," she said. Without "amps," or electrical power, the shuttle would quickly become a high-tech coffin.

"I've got multiple malfs here," John reported.

"Cabin air vent is out, too," added Crip.

All the systems powered by fuel cell two were failing at once! The oxygen malf would have to wait.

"Power down all nonvital systems," Crip ordered.

To save power, the astronauts quickly clicked off switches and other controls. But that wasn't enough. The crew needed vital fuel cell two systems to stay alive—namely, cabin air and water. Those systems were dead or dying.

"Bus-tie," Crip said. "Pronto!"

The crew raced to tie the dead and dying systems to the "busses," or sockets, linked to fuel cells one and three. As Sally worked on the air vent controls, she suddenly spotted three "nits," or minor problems, on the neighboring panel. How long had *those* pesky problems been there?

"Switching water-cooling loop to backup," Sally announced, punching a button. She heard a flurry of clicks and beeps behind her as John, Crip, and Rick rerouted other systems.

"The juice is flowing!" John reported.

"Vital systems back online," Sally confirmed.

"How about that oxygen?" Crip asked Rick.

"I restarted the oxygen and got no joy," Rick replied. "Got no joy" is astronaut lingo for "It didn't work."

Sally knew right away what a faulty oxygen system meant. The malfs and nits were winning.

"Mission abort," Crip said, steadily. An abort was dead serious, a last resort.

The space shuttle was past the point in orbit for landing at a NASA base. Its path and speed left only one place to touch down on solid ground.

"Anyone up for a luau?" Crip asked. "We're gonna shoot for Hawaii."

"Aloha," confirmed Sally and John at the same time.

Crip punched in a computer code, and the shuttle slowly entered the atmosphere.

Sally watched the altitude and speed gauges drop. "Get set for a hairy landing," she told herself. With luck, the shuttle would touch down in Honolulu in twenty-five minutes, but it needed a half mile of pavement to land safely. Airport runways were far too short.

"Ready for roll reversal," said Crip. A roll reversal was a wide, curvy turn that slowed the shuttle's speed.

A smooth carpet of blue, the Pacific Ocean, stretched to the horizon. As far as Sally could see, it was *all* ocean. Where was Hawaii?

"Speed brakes to a hundred percent," Crip said. Speed brakes were big flaps on the tail that, when open, created air resistance to slow down the shuttle.

"Speed brakes a hundred percent," confirmed Sally.

"Ready for roll reversal," said Rick.

As the shuttle swerved again, the speed and altitude readings dropped even faster.

"Just five minutes to touchdown," Sally thought. She tried to keep her heart from pounding. "Use that fear," she told herself. "Use it to stay alert."

"Speed brakes 65 percent," Crip said, as he pushed the brake handle backward. "I got no joy."

"Speed brakes still a hundred percent," Sally confirmed.

Crip tried the handle again. The brakes were still jammed. Another malfunction! Impossible!

"If we switch from auto to manual and back, the brakes might unjam," Sally suggested.

"Roger," Rick agreed. "Switching to manual. Back to auto."

"No go," said Sally. "Speed brakes still a hundred percent."

"We need more speed to reach luau-land," Crip said, simply. "We're not gonna get it without killing those brakes."

"Roger that," Rick agreed.

"I've got a visual," said Rick, pointing to a chain of green and brown islands on the blue carpet below.

"Affirmative," replied Crip. "Landing gear down."

Crip moved the speed brake handle up and back. Still no luck. "Way too slow," he said, shaking his head.

An airplane pilot could pull up, circle around, and try another landing. But the space shuttle was a glider, not a flier. It floated down from the sky like an oversized paper airplane. If it came in too high, too low, too fast, or too slow for a landing, tough luck. There was no second chance.

"We'll have to ditch in the ocean," Crip said matter-of-factly.

Ditching was a tricky emergency landing in water. The pilot had to set down the plane gently and smoothly so that it surfed on top of the water instead of cracking apart. Airplane pilots sometimes ditch their planes in do-or-die situations. Some of them even survive. But no pilot, not even Crip, had ever ditched a space shuttle.

"Landing gear up," Crip said. The shuttle's belly had to be surfboard smooth.

Sally looked through the small window to Crip's left. The ocean seemed to rush up to meet them, rather than the other way around.

"Think there might be an aircraft carrier down there?" said Rick, in a keep-your-chin-up spirit.

"Sure, and maybe some surfers to open the door," Sally replied.

"Nice day for a swim," Crip added grimly. "Over and out."

The window went blank. The shuttle crashed right into the Pacific Ocean and broke into pieces.

There was no chance of survivors.

Four members of the STS-7 crew standing on the steps leading into the motion-based Shuttle Mission Simulator (SMS); left to right, Robert L. Crippen, John M. Fabian, Frederick H. Hauck, and Sally K. Ride. (UPI / Corbis-Bettmann.)

2

A GOOD DAY TO CRASH

Sally, Crip, Rick, and John let loose a nervous laugh. They were all alive. In fact, the crew never left the ground.

The mission was a simulation, a practice flight programmed into a computer. The rehearsal took place in a model of the shuttle cockpit that looked amazingly like the real thing. The window even showed graphics of the stars and earth as they would appear in a real shuttle.

Astronaut trainers sat in the next room during the sim, the nickname for simulation. With fiendish delight, they created all the malfs and nits at will. To jam the speed brakes, a trainer simply touched a light pen to a computer panel and a warning light flashed on Sally's instruments.

Sally turned to John and said, "One way you know you're in a sim and not the real shuttle is that all the abort buttons are worn out."

"Roger that," John replied, smiling.

As the crew joined the trainers, Sally made a mental list of all the malfs during the sim. "A jammed speed brake I can buy," she said. "But a faulty oxygen system, a bad cooling loop, a fire... Wasn't all that a bit much?"

A trainer shrugged and reminded Sally, "Anything that could go wrong on a mission, we can make go wrong."

The trainers had to be tough on astronauts. Sims were the only way to learn how to fly a shuttle. Beginning airplane pilots flew planes over and over with an instructor sitting next to them. But the shuttle had flown just six times, with no instructors aboard. Sally's mission was only STS-7, Space Transportation System flight seven.

Commander Crippen's total experience amounted to hundreds of hours of sims and one real flight, the very first space shuttle flight two years earlier, in 1981. The rest of the crew, including a late addition named Norm Thagard, were space rookies. After a year of training, the five astronauts felt confident they could solve any problem together. At least, that's the way they felt before crashing into the Pacific Ocean.

Sally suddenly realized what that crash-and-die sim was all about. It was John Young's way of reminding the crew that space was a very dangerous place. Better to "crash and die" today in a sim than tomorrow in space. The real lift-off was just days away.

John had piloted Gemini and Apollo missions in the early days of the space program. He also commanded the first space shuttle flight, with Crip as his copilot. Now, John's job was to make sure today's astronauts knew what they were doing. That knowledge included a very clear understanding of the life-and-death risk they were about to take.

"Good job," John said to the crew.

Fatal Space Accidents

JANUARY 27, 1967, Fire on Board: At the end of a long day of system checks, *Apollo 1* astronauts Gus Grissom, Ed White, and Roger Chaffee were sealed inside the capsule for a final test. As part of the test, the capsule was flooded with pure oxygen. A frayed wire created a few sparks, normally no big deal. But on contact with the oxygen, the sparks exploded into a wall of fire, killing all three astronauts in seconds.

APRIL 22, 1967, Major Malfunction: The *Soyuz 1* spacecraft crashed to earth, killing its sole cosmonaut, Vladimir Komarov. (*Cosmonaut*, or "universe sailor," is the Russian term for *astronaut*, or "star sailor.") A system malfunction prevented Komarov from steering his spacecraft properly.

JUNE 30, 1971, Faulty Thruster: When the computer-controlled *Soyuz 11* spacecraft brought its three cosmonauts back to earth, the recovery team found that all three men were dead. A faulty thruster (gas jet) had blasted a hole in the *Soyuz*. All the cabin air had escaped into space.

The Challenger *Disaster*

On January 28, 1986, 73 seconds after lift-off, the *Challenger* space shuttle exploded. All seven crew members died. A nation mourned, especially for Christa McAuliffe, a school teacher. Sally Ride also grieved for the six astronauts who were close friends: Judy Resnik, Michael Smith, Ellison Onizuka, Gregory Jarvis, Ron McNair, and Dick Scobee.

Ride helped to investigate the cause of the accident. Video images showed a strange, orange flash on the shuttle at launch time. For months, workers collected pieces of the shuttle that had sunk to the ocean bottom. Engineers examined each piece closely until they found proof of the accident's cause. A seal called an O-ring cracked due to freezing temperatures the night before launch. The broken seal let two types of fuel mix. The unstable mixture exploded.

After the *Challenger* accident, Sally Ride stated that shuttle flights were not safe for astronauts, let alone civilians such as Christa McAuliffe. She told a reporter for the *Los Angeles Times,* "[The time for sending civilians] has yet to come. It may be decades. The shuttle is an amazingly high-tech and risky vehicle. It's occupied by professionals for a reason."

After improvements were made, Ride agreed that the risk of space flight was once again acceptable—for astronauts, not civilians. In a 1999 interview, she stated,

"Space travel is still a very risky business and will be for quite some time, certainly when today's kids are astronauts. Astronauts understand the risk. [During lift-off,] you're sitting on an explosion. Not much has to go wrong for something to go *really* wrong."

The explosion of the space shuttle Challenger, *January 28, 1986. (NASA.)*

"Sure, if you like talking to ghosts," joked Sally.

As a scientist, Sally once thought failure meant a

Test Pilots

Astronauts of the 1960s and 1970s were some of the best test pilots in the country. Military test pilots are trained by the U.S. Air Force and U.S. Navy to fly new aircraft. First, the pilots learn how to fly in simulators, copies of aircraft cockpits that stay on the ground. Then they take to the air with instructors, who teach how to take off, land, and handle emergencies.

Once these pilots become expert fliers, they are ready to fly new aircraft to see if the machines have any problems. The pilots make fast turns, steep climbs, and nose dives. They roll upside down and right side up over and over at a dizzying pace. Sometimes, a part malfunctions or breaks. Later, engineers will fix the aircraft's faulty design. But right now, the pilot is several miles sky-high in a very fast jet that doesn't work.

In some cases, a small, planned explosion can eject the pilot out of the cockpit. If the blast doesn't seriously hurt the pilot, he or she can parachute to the ground. Not all pilots make it. Test pilots put their lives on the line each time they step into a cockpit.

botched experiment. Now she knew her life depended on millions of shuttle parts *not* failing. With that many parts, chances were high that at least one of them *would* fail.

"Interesting idea to ditch the shuttle," John said to Crip. "I'd love to see you pull that off for real."

"Hope I never get the chance," Crip replied, smiling.

Crip was used to facing death. So was John Young. Both men had been test pilots for the military. In flight after flight, they put their lives on the line to fly the fastest, newest jets in the world.

In the early 1960s, many people at NASA thought that scientists shouldn't, wouldn't, or couldn't take that life-and-death risk. Even more people, in and out of NASA, thought women astronauts were out of the question. Those people just couldn't picture a woman dying in space.

"It wasn't part of the social order," astronaut John Glenn had said.

For years, NASA hired only male test pilots. But now, in 1983, getting into space and making it back alive was no longer enough. The new goal was to get into space and do something useful, such as launch a satellite and conduct experiments. To reach that goal, NASA needed some of the smartest, bravest scientists in the country—men *and* women.

Sally Ride was clearly smart enough. She had the highest college degree, a doctorate, in the science of physics. Was Sally brave enough to be a space pioneer? Would she stay cool and do her job during a real emergency? Could she accept the very real possibility of dying in space?

The next week, on June 18, 1983, the world was about to find out. That clear Saturday morning, millions of people turned on their TVs to watch the launch of mission STS-7. Every launch was special. The space shuttle was new and exciting. But this launch drew one of the biggest crowds in space history. People wanted to see Sally Ride become the first American woman to fly into space. At age 32, Sally would also be the youngest astronaut to reach space.

Dr. Sally K. Ride and the crew of the STS-7 mission depart from the astronaut quarters on their way to the launch complex. (NASA.)

The STS-7 crew walked out of the main building at Kennedy Space Center in Florida. All five astronauts wore matching blue flight suits and black boots. They all smiled and waved for the TV crowd. But the world's eyes were on one astronaut: Sally Ride.

Not that anyone could miss her. The four men were taller and had short haircuts and broad shoulders. Sally, five-feet six-inches short, had a mane of dark, wavy hair. Still smiling, she hopped into the bus that drove astronauts to the launchpad.

"How did it feel to be the first American woman in space?" Sally knew reporters would ask that question after the flight. She didn't want people to think of her as a "woman astronaut." Sally Ride was an astronaut, just like Crip, Rick, John, and Norm. Even so, she'd have to answer that question somehow.

How *did* she feel? Excited, for sure. Thrilled, nervous, a bit scared? All present and accounted for. But Sally felt one thing that her four crewmates didn't feel.

"I've got to be perfect," she told herself. One mistake could cast a shadow on all women astronauts to come. People might say, "See? Women *can't* do it."

The pressure to be perfect didn't faze Sally. It fueled her. It made her even more determined to do her job well. "No, not well," she reminded herself. "Perfect."

As the crew hopped out of the bus onto the launchpad, Sally heard loud hissing and spitting. She looked up and instantly felt like an ant. The rockets, 30 stories high, were getting ready to explode.

An elevator lifted the astronauts to the nose of the space shuttle. There, they crawled through a hatch into the tiny cockpit. Even Sally, the shortest astronaut, had to crouch down as she slipped into her seat behind Crip. The shuttle was sitting on its tail, so the seats faced upward, toward space. The astronauts sat on their backs while technicians strapped them in.

"I'm here," Sally thought. "This is really happening. This time, it's for real."

Sally glanced at the Mission Time Clock. T minus 4 hours. Four long, nail-biting hours to lift-off. That whole time, she'd have to sit in a hard, metal seat. That whole time, millions of pounds of rocket fuel were right next to her. In four hours, all that fuel would explode like a huge bomb. The blast would shoot Sally 200 miles into the sky in minutes.

That's when Sally Kristen Ride, space pioneer, would make history. Sally smiled. To think that, as a girl, space travel had never entered her mind. She dreamed instead of being a major league baseball player!

3

PLAY BALL!

"C'mon Bear," Sally said to her younger sister, Karen. "Hurry up. We've got to get out there before the game starts."

After school, Sally played baseball almost every day. Her sister, Bear, sometimes tagged along, but Sally was the only girl who played. As the sisters stepped outside, Sally checked the weather. Just enough clouds to block the sun. Not too hot. She wet her finger and stuck it in the air. Not much wind, either. Perfect for playing ball. In southern California, Sally could play outside almost every day of the year.

The boys were marking the bases when Sally and Bear showed up. Like other suburbs of Los Angeles, Encino had a ball field. But for whatever reason, playing in an empty lot was more fun.

"Hey, Sally! You're on my team." A blond boy waved her over.

"But are *you* on *my* team, Jimbo?" Sally joked.

She sized up the rest of the boys. Yes, she was the only girl. But Sally fit in with this group like a ball in a well-oiled glove. "A team player," coaches called her.

Bear had another view of her big sister. "Sally's better than all you guys put together," Bear had bragged one day.

No one disagreed. Sally threw hard, hit well, and ran fast. Sally and Jimbo picked the rest of their team. Then they took the field while Bear watched on the sidelines.

Sally pictured herself on L.A.'s new baseball team, the Dodgers. She imagined the makeshift field as the Dodgers' Coliseum stadium. Bear was a roaring crowd. TV cameras captured Sally's spectacular plays.

"Too bad there aren't any lights," Sally mumbled. Too soon, the game ended on account of darkness.

Sally and Bear went home and grabbed a hot dog for dinner. The next morning, their mother saw the two girls off to school.

February 20, 1962. Sally wrote the date neatly at the top of her notebook paper. Then she wrote "Sally" underneath.

"Today," her teacher announced, "an astronaut is going into space."

The whole idea of space travel was brand-new. A man from the Soviet Union went up first. But no one knew anything about him. Then Alan Shepherd went up last May, a few weeks before Sally's tenth birthday. *Everyone* knew who he was.

"Can anyone tell me this astronaut's name?" the teacher asked, scanning the class for hands.

"Oh! Oh!" blurted a boy in the front row. "John Glenn!"

Astronaut John Glenn walks with technicians toward the Friendship Seven *space capsule, February 20, 1962. (© Bettmann-Corbis.)*

The Mercury 7

In the early 1960s, NASA chose seven veteran test pilots, called the Mercury 7, to be the first American astronauts. Alan Shepherd, the first American in space, made his 15-minute 22-second flight on May 5, 1961. The other astronauts included Gus Grissom (later killed in a launchpad accident), John Glenn (the first American to orbit earth), Scott Carpenter, Wally Schirra, Gordon Cooper, and Deke Slayton.

The teacher smiled. "That's right. What's special about John Glenn's flight?"

"He's gonna do an orbit!" the boy said excitedly.

"An orbit, yes," the teacher echoed. "John Glenn is going to be the first American to circle the earth."

The teacher wheeled a large cart into the classroom. On top of it was a black-and-white TV. She clicked on the TV and adjusted the rabbit ears, the antenna, until a snowy picture emerged.

Sally could barely make out the rocket on the small screen. After a couple of minutes, a voice from the TV counted down. "Ten, nine, eight, seven..."

A huge gray cloud filled the bottom of the screen.

"three... two... one..."

The voice paused and then said, "Lift-off! We have lift-off."

A white rocket rose out of the cloud, above the ground. It seemed to move in slow motion. The rocket grew smaller until it finally disappeared from view.

Sally looked at her paper. She wrote four sentences to describe the lift-off, step-by-step. Then she concluded, "Everyone was very happy for the astronaut."

Sally was happy, too, but she was more interested in sports than space travel. Sally's mother had given her a tennis racquet. Hitting a tennis ball, Sally discovered, wasn't all that different than hitting a baseball. With practice, she could hit the ball anywhere she wanted, hard and fast, just like a baseball.

Sally was soon good enough to have a top tennis coach, Alice Marble. Alice had been a national tennis champion four times in the 1950s. She told Sally that she could be the best, if she really wanted it.

Sally wanted it. She joined the junior tennis circuit and played against the toughest players in the country. She was good enough to win a tennis scholarship to the Westlake School for Girls. Famous people went to Westlake. Los Angeles was, after all, the home of Hollywood. But Sally had no desire to be famous. The attention of fans at tennis tournaments made her uneasy. Sally just wanted to play her game.

In her junior year at Westlake, Sally met a teacher who changed her life. Dr. Elizabeth Mommaerts taught science. Not many girls were interested in science, and as a result, not many women became scientists. Dr. Mommaerts was an exception.

"I need a volunteer," Dr. Mommaerts said one day. "Who likes to run?"

"I'll do it!" Sally said.

The teacher smiled. "Okay, Sally, let me take your pulse."

Dr. Mommaerts placed two fingers on the inside of Sally's wrist. She looked at her watch for exactly 15 sec-

Who Is a Scientist?

Dr. Maria Goeppert Mayer in the 1960s. (UPI / Corbis-Bettmann.)

In your mind, picture a scientist. What image do you see?

Perhaps your scientist is wearing a white lab coat. A lot of scientists do. The coat protects clothes and skin from spilled chemicals. Maybe your scientist's hair is frizzy and wild, like Albert Einstein's. Does he have thick glasses? Does he act a little weird or even "mad"? Is he awkward at parties?

onds and then said, "Sixty beats a minute. That's pretty good.

"Okay, Sally, let's see how that pulse jumps after a little exercise." Dr. Mommaerts held up a stopwatch and said, "Go!"

Sally ran around the gym until Dr. Mommaerts clicked the stopwatch and said, "Stop." The teacher took

Picture a beaker of bubbly liquid in your scientist's hand and the stereotype is complete. A stereotype is an overly simple, general description of a group of people. It is usually wrong.

Does this woman (left) look like a scientist to you? She's nothing like the *stereotype* just described. Her name is Maria Goeppert Mayer (1906–1972). She won a Nobel Prize, the top science honor, in 1963 for discovering part of the structure of an atom.

Mayer taught physics at the University of California in San Diego, where Sally Ride teaches now. Mayer, Dr. Elizabeth Mommaerts (Ride's science teacher), and Sally Ride all break the stereotype mold just by being themselves. Today, Sally Ride is not only a scientist but also a speaker, a pilot, a tennis player, a photographer, a book author, and a fan of William Shakespeare!

Who is a scientist really like? Anybody and everybody—including you!

Sally's pulse again. "Sixty-four?" she said with surprise. "Sally, you're in great shape. Most people would be in the nineties."

Sally smiled. Dr. Mommaert's words made her feel like a tennis champ already. She pictured herself in a crisp, white tennis dress on center court at Wimbledon, one of the world's top tournaments; Sally Kristen Ride versus Billie Jean King, the number one player in the world.

"Soon to be number two," Sally thought, as she mentally slammed a shot down the line.

4

A TENNIS SHOT AND A MOON SHOT

On Sunday, July 20, 1969, Sally Ride was competing in a national tennis tournament. It wasn't Wimbledon, but it was an important step in that direction. Sally was in Wilmington, Delaware, vying to be the best 18-and-under player in the United States. Talk about the thrill of a lifetime!

That same day, three men were about to have the thrill of *their* lifetimes. *Apollo 11* astronauts Neil Armstrong and Buzz Aldrin were about to land on the moon in the *Eagle,* a lunar landing vehicle. Their pilot, Michael Collins, would orbit the moon in the *Apollo* spaceship.

Everyone was talking about it. "The Event of the Century," the TV newscasters dubbed it. No human had ever set foot on the moon before. Until just a few years ago, many people thought it was just a fantasy.

The astronauts had TV cameras that beamed video and audio from the moon to earth. Earthlings couldn't get enough.

"Hey, we could rig up a TV set near the courts," suggested one tennis player.

"Great idea," Sally joked. "Then we can hit tennis shots while we watch the moon shot. A little white ball on the court, a big white ball in space—what's the difference?"

The idea was nixed, of course. A national junior tennis tournament is too important. The top players usually turn pro.

Around 4 o'clock, the *Eagle* separated from the *Apollo* and fell gently to the moon's surface. Sally missed the historic moment because she was playing in a tough match. She won the first set, lost the second set, and in the final set hit a screaming down-the-line shot to win the match.

Sally called Bear to report that she was still alive, but barely, tenniswise.

According to Bear, the lunar landing was a close call, too. "It was really something," Bear said. "The TV guy said Armstrong's heart was beating twice as fast as it should."

"Wow," Sally said. "What happened?"

"I'm not sure," Bear said. "It all happened in, like, ten minutes. One guy said the *Eagle* was about to land on a boulder. Armstrong had to fly the thing over to another landing spot. He just made it before fuel ran out."

"But everything's cool, right?" Sally asked.

"Sure," Bear said. " 'The *Eagle* has landed,' just like Armstrong said. Now they're sitting inside, waiting to come out."

It was a long wait—six and a half hours. Sally had an early-morning match the next day, but she decided to stay up late and watch the big moment. That evening, she and a few other players sat around a state-of-the-art color TV. Not everybody had color TVs. They were new and expensive.

"Hey, we'll be able to see all that red, white, and blue in living color," Sally joked.

All the space missions were painted in patriotic colors. Even the people on the ground at Mission Control waved American flags when something good happened.

Sally turned a big dial to the "on" position and waited for the picture to appear. A fuzzy, color image emerged slowly on the small screen.

Sally moved the rabbit ears until the picture cleared up a little. There on the screen was President Richard Nixon watching the astronauts on *his* TV.

Sally wanted to see astronauts, not presidents. She turned a dial with numbers on it. It clicked from 2 to 4 to 7. All three channels had the same picture, live from NASA TV.

The TV picture finally switched from the White House to the inside of the *Eagle*. Neil Armstrong was wearing a bulky, white spacesuit with a big pack on the back. Pockets, instruments, and straps covered his chest. An American flag was sewn onto his left shoulder. The flag was black and white. The astronauts didn't even have color TV!

Everyone stared at the screen and waited for the big moment. At exactly 10:39 p.m. the hatch of the *Eagle* opened. Armstrong backed out of the lander in slow motion.

It took 17 full minutes for him to climb down the metal rungs.

The room fell silent. Sally held her breath. Armstrong jumped off the last rung and fell several feet to the lander's footpad. Then he firmly planted his left boot on the surface of the moon.

Everyone cheered.

"Cool!" Sally said. A man was actually walking on the moon!

"That's one small step for man, and one giant leap for mankind." Those words were famous as soon as they left the astronaut's lips. The TV announcers kept repeating them.

Man. Mankind. From that moment on, boys all over the world yearned to be astronauts, just like Neil Armstrong.

The astronaut's voice crackled over the TV again. "The surface is fine and powdery... I can pick it up loosely with my toe."

Armstrong reached down and grabbed a handful of dust. He put it into a pocket in his suit. "The grab sample," the TV reporters called it. If Armstrong had to get off the moon fast, at least he'd have a souvenir for the scientists at home.

Armstrong's camera panned Tranquillity Base, the landing site. *Tranquil* means calm and peaceful. But the moon was more like flat and lifeless. The gray, rock-strewn and cratered surface dropped abruptly into a sea of black at the horizon. The horizon looked impossibly close. It seemed like the astronauts could step right off the moon and into space.

At 11:11 p.m. Buzz Aldrin planted his space boots on the

moon. Aldrin's shadow was sharp, black, and long, Sally noted. That meant the sun was low, and without air or clouds to filter it, very bright.

The two astronauts bounced and hopped around like big, white beach balls. The bootprints they left behind looked jarringly out of place on the dusty ground.

Sally did a quick mental calculation. Because of the moon's weaker gravity, a 180-pound astronaut weighed just 30 pounds there, maybe double that with a heavy spacesuit on. Still, 60 pounds was light enough to lift.

Buzz Aldrin set up a big aluminum sheet.

"That collects solar wind," Sally explained.

The group looked at her in surprise.

"Solar wind?" a player asked. "I thought there wasn't any air in space."

"There isn't," Sally replied. "The solar wind is a stream of particles from the sun—bits of electrified gas. That aluminum sheet traps them like flypaper so that scientists can study them back on earth."

Armstrong's voice crackled over the TV again. He read the plaque on the lunar lander. "Here men from the planet earth first set foot upon the moon, July 1969 A.D. We came in peace for all mankind."

Men. Mankind.

Sally's mind wandered back to tennis. She had a tournament to win, and it was almost midnight. She started to get up, but a player said, "Wait, Sally! They haven't planted the flag yet. That's the best part!"

Sally suddenly felt unpatriotic. She sat back down. "I

Astronaut Buzz Aldrin standing beside the American flag on the surface of the moon during the Apollo 11 *EVA. (NASA.)*

guess if we all stay up late, we'll be even on the court tomorrow," she said.

The flag planting *did* turn out to be a big deal. The TV people really played it up. But Sally noticed something strange.

"That flag looks weird," she said, "It wouldn't fly like that on the moon."

"Like what?" a player asked.

"Straight out like that. It would droop down, like a flag

on a calm day." Sally figured NASA rigged it up with wires or something.

It was early morning before Sally finally got to sleep. When she woke up a few hours later, the astronauts were bouncing around the moon again. And Sally still had a tough match to play. She lost, but not because she was tired. Her opponent was just plain better.

Sally ranked among the top 20 junior players in the country, but she wanted to be the best. Three years later, in 1972, Billie Jean King thought Sally could do it. Sally met the number-one player in the world at a tennis tournament.

BACK TO THE MOON?

Twelve American men walked on the moon. The last Apollo moon mission ended on December 19, 1972. For the rest of the 20th century, no human being set foot on the moon again.

In the late 1990s, a space probe named *Clementine* made an astounding discovery. It found evidence of water ice at the moon's south pole. The ice was at the bottom of craters, where the sun never shines.

The existence of water makes the moon a much more hospitable place for humans. We need water to drink, of course. But water can also be turned into hydrogen rocket fuel, oxygen, and electricity. So also in the late 1990s, robotic space probes began searching for suitable sites for a future moon colony.

The life of a professional tennis player looked tempting. It wasn't so much the money. Sally liked to compete—and to win. Competition made her play better. It pushed her skills to the limit.

Sally then played on the Stanford University team in Palo Alto, California. But after a few years against some of the best players in the country, Sally knew her game wasn't solid enough to be a top pro. Tennis, she decided, was not in the stars.

So what career *was* in Sally's stars?

CHAPTER 5

THE BE-ALL AND END-ALL

"Cool!" Sally said, after the laser test. There was no other word for it.

She was used to flashlight beams that spread out and faded. The laser beam traveled in a straight line that never seemed to end. It looked like a red, glowing string.

Sally had decided to become a scientist in order to discover things that no one else knew. And few people knew what laser beams could do or how they worked. Lasers had been invented only a dozen years ago, in 1960. They were newer than space travel.

"Newer than me, too," Sally thought. She was born in 1951.

New is good to a young scientist, exciting even. It means there is lots of room for exploring and discovering. Who knew how scientists would use lasers in the future?

Already, a laser beam had measured the exact distance between the earth and moon. That distance changes because the moon doesn't orbit earth in a perfect circle.

To make the laser test possible, Apollo astronauts had put a mirror on the moon. A scientist on earth aimed a laser at the mirror. The laser beam bounced off the mirror and returned to earth. The farther away the moon was in its orbit, the longer it took the laser beam to go and return. Of course, when dealing with the speed of light, "long" is a relative term. The whole experiment took a couple of seconds.

Amazing Lasers

Today, laser beams are used to
- Make precise cuts in cloth
- Make very fine incisions (cuts) during surgery
- Burn away tumors (abnormal growths in the body)
- Weld metal machine parts
- Scan CDs, bar codes, and other computer devices
- Etch (carve) tiny circuits in computer chips
- Carry computer data long distances over "light pipes" called optical fibers
- Trigger nuclear fusion (the combining of atoms to turn matter into energy)

Sally also had fun with electrons, protons, and neutrons—the parts of an atom. These subatomic particles are far too small to see. Yet Sally was one of the few people on earth who knew how they acted. She figured out their mass and energy and motion in equations. Take Albert Einstein's famous $e=mc^2$: energy *(e)* equals mass *(m)* times the speed of light *(c)* squared. The speed of light in meters per second squared is mind-boggling: 89,875,518,000,000,000, more or less.

"Equations and more equations," Sally said to her roommate, Molly. "I love science, but I need a break from all those numbers."

Molly was an English major. She suggested Sally take a literature class.

"Okay, let's see what turns you on," Sally said, reaching for Molly's book. Molly was reading *Macbeth*, a play by William Shakespeare.

Sally whistled. "Shakespeare. Not too shabby," she said.

Shakespeare was the greatest playwright in England and perhaps the world. Because he wrote four hundred years ago, his version of the English language was tough for modern people to read. Sally cracked open the book and read the first line:

FIRST WITCH: *When shall we meet again?*
In thunder, lightning, or in rain?

"Piece of cake," Sally said, and then read the next line.

SECOND WITCH: *When the hurly-burly's done,*

When the battle's lost and won.

"Hurly-burly?" asked Sally.

"A poetic word for fighting," replied Molly. "Scotland is at war, and Macbeth is one of the warriors."

Sally skipped ahead.

MACBETH: *If it were done when 'tis done, then 'twere well It were done quickly.*

"Huh?" She read it again. "Still makes no sense."

"Macbeth is talking about murdering the king," Molly explained. "He's not sure if he wants to go ahead with it. But if he does, he wants to get it over quickly."

Sally nodded and continued.

MACBETH:... *that this blow Might be the be-all and the end-all, here.*

"Be-all and end-all," repeated Sally. "I've heard that phrase before. So murdering the king will solve everything."

"Or so Macbeth thinks," Molly said. "All it does is create lots of new problems—more murders, actually."

Sally was hooked. She read the first two acts that evening.

"It's like solving a puzzle," she observed. "You have to figure out what he's trying to say and find all the little clues that show you're right."

Molly laughed. "Shakespeare as read by a scientist. To me, it's just great drama and poetry."

Sally's English papers were scientific, too: short, to-the-point, and logical. Not a word was wasted. Molly's papers, by contrast, focused on the characters' passions and emotions. Both Molly and Sally got good grades, but Sally realized not everyone saw the world the same way she did.

Sally Ride on the campus of Stanford University in the 1970s. (© Bettmann-Corbis.)

Molly and Sally were different in other ways, too. One day, Sally's truck broke down in scorching heat in the middle of nowhere. Molly curled up in the back seat for a nap, waiting for help to come along. Sally couldn't stand the thought of wasting a day doing nothing. So she popped open the hood.

"The radiator overheated," Sally reported to Molly. "Probably has a hole in it."

WOMEN IN SCIENCE

Since Sally Ride's school days, the number of women earning science degrees has more than doubled (see chart). Most of these women earn degrees in biology, medicine, and psychology (the science of the mind) rather than in physics, Sally Ride's field. In 1995, fewer than one out of four scientists were women.

PERCENTAGE OF SCIENCE AND ENGINEERING GRADUATES WHO WERE WOMEN

	Bachelor's (B.S.)	Master's (M.S.)	Doctorate (Ph.D.)
1966	24%	13%	8%
1995	46%	38%	31%

SOURCE: National Science Foundation, Division of Science Resources Studies, *Women, Minorities, and Persons with Disabilities in Science and Engineering: 1998.*

In her trunk Sally found a saucepan and a roll of tape. She sealed the radiator hole with gobs of tape. Then she took off with the saucepan to find water to refill the radiator. An hour later, Sally and Molly were on their way.

Sally graduated from Stanford University in 1973 with two degrees: physics and English. The English department had far more women. Women science majors were an endangered species.

Sally didn't mind. She was used to "playing ball" with the boys. If anyone told her she couldn't, she just flipped a mental switch marked OBLIVIOUS and paid no attention. In fact, Sally chose to become even more of an endangered species. She decided to get the be-all and end-all of college degrees, a Ph.D. in physics. Most women science majors chose biology, the study of plants and animals.

"What happened to Shakespeare?" asked Molly.

"I thought about it," Sally confessed. "But I like science more. In fact, my life is set. I know exactly what I want."

"To be a housewife?" Molly joked. "Have six kids?"

"Yeah, right," Sally said. "I'm going into research. Then I'll get a job here at Stanford."

"Wow, let me write this down," said Molly, pretending to scribble. "Sally Ride, physics graduate in 1973. Sally Ride, physics professor in 1977. What a leap."

Sally laughed. "It does sound kinda programmed..."

"But it's nice to know what you want," conceded Molly. "Let all the number of the stars give light to thy fair way."

"*Julius Caesar?*" Sally guessed—correctly.

By 1977, Sally's plan was right on track. She had her

degrees—a bachelor's, a master's, and soon, a Ph.D. Then in an instant, her life changed. "All the number of the stars" lit up a whole new track in the form of a small ad in the college newspaper.

"Cool!" Sally shouted to no one and everyone around. "I can't believe it!"

Sally read the ad again... and again. NASA was seeking scientists to join the Astronaut Corps, women included! Women, in fact, were invited to apply, said the ad.

"I'm doin' it!" Sally said, grinning. "I'm gonna be an astronaut!"

6

ONE IN
A MILLION

Sally reached for her desk calculator. Eight thousand, three hundred, and seventy people wanted to be astronauts. NASA had 35 slots. Only one out of every 250 would make it.

"Forget about the numbers," Sally said aloud, pushing the calculator aside. "If I make it, *when* I make it, I'll be one in a million."

On a planet of several billion people, only a few dozen men—and one woman—had flown into space. The woman was Valentina Tereshkova, a Russian who orbited earth in 1963.

One thousand, two hundred, and fifty-one women had applied to be astronauts. But Sally wasn't thinking about being the next woman in space. She was thinking about flying into space, period.

Her parents, Joyce and Dale Ride, were thrilled.

"They know what an astronaut does," Sally said to Bear. "I'm not sure they could really picture those atomic particles."

"Neither could I," Bear replied. Bear was now a minister. Like Sally, she chose a field that few women entered. "What made you decide to do it?"

"To be honest, Bear, I'm not really sure," Sally said. "All

The Astronaut Corps

The Johnson Space Center (JSC) near Houston, Texas, is the home of Mission Control, the ground crew that supports piloted space flights. The NASA base is also where astronauts work and live. The Astronaut Corps is the group currently in training for space missions. Astronaut candidates, or ascans, are men and women learning how to be astronauts.

In 1999, almost one out of five active astronauts were women. By far, most women become mission specialists, astronauts who conduct experiments, fix satellites in space, and perform other important duties. Fewer women are pilots, astronauts who fly the space shuttle. After gaining experience in space, some pilots become commanders, or mission leaders, like Robert Crippen.

Think of it this way: Pilots take the shuttle up and down; specialists make the trip worthwhile by advancing science and technology in space.

I know is that I was running out the door to apply before I even finished reading that ad."

"Sort of like a calling," Bear commented. "I'll be praying for you, Sally."

"Thanks for your vote, Bear," Sally said. "That's one down and all of NASA to go."

"No problem," said Bear. "Sally, you're in great shape.

A view of the Mission Operations Control Room of the Johnson Space Center. (NASA.)

You're great at science. You get along with the boys... excuse me, the men. NASA will love you."

"Oh yeah, and you studied Shakespeare," Bear added.

"What's that got to do with it?" Sally asked. "I doubt too many English majors applied for the job."

"It proves you're not a science nerd," Bear said. "If you can tackle both physics and Shakespeare, you can handle any subject."

Sally began to get an eerie feeling. "You know, now that I think about it, I've been preparing to be an astronaut all my life. I just didn't know it until now."

A few months later, Sally learned that she made the first cut. She was now one of 208 candidates. She had won out over *thousands* of other people.

Sally flew down to Houston, Texas, in October of 1977 for a week of interviews and tests. Her first look at Johnson Space Center (JSC) made her feel right at home. It looked like a college campus: bright, white buildings around an open, parklike center. The park even had a little duck pond.

The "professors" were NASA trainers—lots of them. Like movie stars, astronauts get all the fame and glory. But anyone who visits JSC learns the truth. Hundreds of people work behind the scenes. Make that thousands of people, if you count all the people who build the spacecraft.

After dropping her belongings in a dorm-style room, Sally reviewed her schedule. She began to feel like a soldier. The times were in military notation—14:42, for example, is 2:42 in the afternoon. They were also down to the minute.

"The only thing missing are bathroom breaks," Sally joked to her roommate, Janet.

"There's a one-minute break between the briefing and the medical check," Janet noted, smiling, "but we'll need that minute to cross the campus."

Sally laughed. "Guess we better do our business now, then."

"That's how it'll be in space," Janet added.

"What will be?" Sally asked. "No bathroom breaks?"

"The schedule. They program almost every minute of time so we're too busy to get homesick or bored," Janet explained.

"That makes sense. I'm sure NASA wants to get its money's worth while we're up there."

Both Sally and Janet expected to make it. Confidence, ambition, and a positive attitude—those were clearly three of the requirements.

The two women stepped out of the air-conditioned building into a blast of hot air. It felt like a hair dryer was pointing directly at their faces.

"If this is Texas in October, summertime must be a sauna," Janet said.

"I guess this weather is part of the conditioning," Sally joked.

At the first briefing, Sally looked around the room at the others in her group. They were mostly men, she noted, and three women, including herself and Janet. The third woman was a pretty blonde with her hair rolled neatly in a bun. Her nametag said RHEA.

Sally's eye caught a tall redhead named Steve who looked about her age. At 27, she was one of the youngest. Most of the finalists were in their thirties and forties.

A few men had crew cuts. Sally guessed they were military pilots. But most of the men sported shaggier haircuts and sideburns—the new style. The Apollo astronauts looked like clones compared to this group.

Speaking of which, astronaut John Young began the briefing. He talked about what it was like to be an astronaut. The fun, the fame, the hard work... no surprises there. Then John mentioned "the media microscope." Reporters examine every iota of an astronaut's life. They ask the same mind-numbing questions again and again. Every flaw or flub gets magnified and broadcast coast to coast.

Sally began to feel uneasy. She had talked to plenty of sports reporters, but college tennis players and national heroes weren't quite in the same media universe.

Next, a trainer gave an overview of the training. Then Eugene Kranz spoke. He was in charge of Mission Control during the Apollo years.

"In space, high-tech accidents are unavoidable and unpredictable," he said seriously. Then he recounted all the malfunctions that nearly killed Apollo astronauts. During *Apollo 12,* for example, lightning knocked out electrical systems just after lift-off. With quick thinking, astronaut Al Bean restored power and the crew achieved orbit. Al was now a leader in the astronaut training program.

Missing from the list of mishaps was the *Apollo 1*

tragedy. Three astronauts died in a launchpad fire with no chance of escaping. "No chance," Sally guessed, was the reason Kranz didn't bring it up. Astronaut training dealt only with solvable problems. Why talk about things you can't do anything about?

George Abbey spoke next. Along with John Young and a few others, he would pick the new group of astronauts from among the finalists. George said the schedule told finalists what to do and where to do it, but no one could tell them *how* to do it. There was no "right way" or "wrong way" to answer questions or pass tests, he said.

"Just do your best and let us worry about the rest," George said.

As an athlete, Sally was used to going head-to-head, win or lose. Now, she felt less like an athlete and more like an actor trying out for a part. An actor might be able to sing, dance, and do somersaults well, but none of that mattered if the director needed cartwheels.

Likewise, NASA directors needed astronauts to do certain jobs. They looked for people who did those jobs extremely well.

Sally took a good, long look around the room. These people were all brainy, they all wanted to be astronauts, and they all usually succeeded in reaching their goals. Who would be picked for the part?

7

MEDICAL MALFUNCTIONS

For the next seven days, doctors poked and prodded Sally. Was her blood pressure too high? Did her heart beat strongly and regularly? Were the blood and urine tests normal? One "medical malfunction," or health problem, could easily knock her out of the running.

For one test, Sally jogged on a treadmill while wearing an oxygen mask. The doctors measured how much oxygen her body needed during exercise. The less oxygen she needed, the better shape she was in.

Another test involved a round, canvas bag about two and a half feet in diameter. The Space Rescue Ball looked more like an oversized beach ball. In a space emergency, astronauts were supposed to squeeze their bodies inside it. The ball would protect them for a short time if the cabin depressurized—that is, lost its air.

For now, the Space Ball had a different purpose. It was used for testing claustrophobia, the fear of enclosed spaces. Phobias were another reason to knock people off the list.

Sally glanced up at Steve Hawley.

"For once, the short folks have it easier," he said, smiling.

Sally smiled as she unzipped the ball and climbed in. She strapped on an oxygen tank and mask. Then she bent her head to her knees so that Steve could zip the ball closed. Inside the canvas cocoon, Sally felt cramped but, to her relief, not claustrophobic. She relaxed while she waited for the signal to emerge. Then she calmly stepped out of the ball.

"What's next?" Steve asked, looking over Sally's shoulder at the schedule.

"Shrink time," Sally smiled, twirling her finger around her ear in a "crazy" signal.

Sally had never been to a "shrink," the nickname for a psychologist. She knew she wasn't "crazy," but she didn't like the idea of a stranger asking personal questions. She pictured a long couch in a stuffy room full of books. That's what shrink offices looked like in the movies.

Instead, Sally entered a white, bare room with two chairs. She sat in the chair closer to the door. A few minutes later, a woman entered. Her face was pleasant, but without emotion. The doctor started right in.

"How are you?" she asked.

An easy question. People asked that every day. "Just fine, thank you," Sally replied.

The next question came out of left field.

"If you were something other than a human, what would you be?"

"Here we go," thought Sally. She thought for a few seconds and nothing came to mind. "An atom," she said, finally. Atomic physics was, after all, her field of study.

"Do you love your mother?" the doctor asked.

"Of course," answered Sally, this time without hesitation.

The doctor nodded and scribbled. "How do you feel about your sister?"

"Just great. She's terrific."

More scribbling. "Have you ever had amnesia—a loss of memory?"

Sally grinned. "I don't know. I can't remember."

The doctor's face didn't flicker.

"Guess she's heard that joke before," thought Sally.

The doctor asked a few more basic questions and scribbled a few more notes. Her face held no clue as to how well or poorly Sally was doing.

Next, Sally strolled into the office of a second psychologist. This doctor showed plenty of emotion—a stern scowl. Her gaze bore through Sally like a laser beam. "Dr. Laser Beam," Sally decided to call her.

"Hi, I'm..." Sally started to say.

"Five, seven, four, one, three!" Dr. Laser Beam said out of the blue. "Now, say that backward!"

Sally blinked in surprise. Then she replied calmly, "Three, one, four, seven, five."

"Name the number you left out!" ordered Dr. Laser Beam.

"Left out?" Sally asked. She was sure she said all the numbers. But before she could answer, the doctor barked another startling question.

"Name five American presidents!"

"Washington, Lincoln, Kennedy, um, Ford, and..."

"...Again! Alphabetically!"

"Ford, Kennedy, Lincoln, Washington..."

"Who's after Washington!"

"But..." Sally started to say.

"Name everything you ate yesterday," barked the doctor.

Sally took a deep breath. Dr. Laser Beam was not going to let up. "Just do the best you can," Sally told herself. "Don't sweat over it."

After a few more bizarre questions, Sally's time was up. As she walked out of the room, she shrugged at the next "victim." That afternoon, she asked one of the astronauts what that second shrink was all about.

"Being cool, calm, and collected under pressure," he answered. "She was trying to rattle you so that you couldn't think straight."

"I get it," said Sally, "crazy questions to make you go crazy."

At the end of the week, the last hurdle was the final interview. Ten men sat at a long table. Sally sat in a chair facing them. She knew some of the faces, including George Abbey and John Young. Each man had a folder—a copy of her file, Sally guessed. Her whole life, and now her whole future, was in that file.

"Hot enough for you?" said George. His friendly tone instantly made Sally relax. Small talk she could handle.

"I haven't melted yet," Sally joked. Most of the men smiled, a good sign.

"Would you consider yourself a tidy person?" one of the interviewers asked.

Sally pictured her apartment in California: wall-to-wall books, papers, and piles of stuff. "I like to know where things are," she said. It wasn't exactly a lie. But in the dozens of interviews, it was the only time she bent the truth.

"Why do you want to be an astronaut?" This question came from John Young.

"To fly into space," Sally replied. It was that simple.

Later that day, Sally packed her bags and returned to California. She would either make the final cut or not. There was nothing she could do about it now. So instead of fretting, Sally concentrated on her work. She had a doctoral degree in astrophysics to finish. By the end of 1977, Sally was no longer Sally Ride. She was Dr. Sally Ride.

"Mission accomplished," Sally thought. "Now what?"

She hadn't heard from NASA in months. Then the phone call finally came on January 16, 1978.

"Sally Ride, this is George Abbey," said a gentle, friendly voice.

Sally's heart thumped. George Abbey himself!

"How's the weather there in California?" George asked.

*Sally Ride at a press conference on January 16,
1978, the day she was selected for the astronaut
training program. (UPI/Corbis-Bettmann.)*

Without missing a beat, Sally replied, "Pretty laid-back,
just the way we Californians like it."

George chuckled and said, "Sally, we've got a job here for
you, if you still are interested in taking it."

"Yes, sir!" Sally answered.

In that instant, Sally Ride knew she was in for the
biggest adventure of her life.

8

HANGING TOUGH

"Let's see," **Sally** *thought.* "Hang on. Hang up. Hang around. Hang nail… Hangman…"

Now she was getting silly. After an hour of hanging in the hot, muggy air, strung up like a puppet, *anyone* would get a little silly.

"Silly Sally. Silly Sally sat on the seashore."

Sally tried to shift her body in the parachute harness. The straps were still too tight. Sally kicked her dangling feet, doing a dance step in the air.

Please let these feet touch the ground soon, she thought.

"Hang tough," Sally said aloud, steeling her mind against boredom, discomfort, and 100-degree heat. The parachute hang was part of the survival-and-rescue training. An emergency landing could strand astronauts for

Sally Ride suspended in a parachute harness during training exercises at survival school, Vance Air Force Base, Oklahoma, 1978. (NASA.)

hours on land or in water. If that happened, Sally definitely wanted to survive and be rescued. She'd hang there all day if that's what it took.

Sally's mind flashed back to the *Apollo 13* mission in 1970. An explosion almost stranded the astronauts in space forever. To save power, Sally recalled, the three men rode home in a lunar lander built for two. They withstood freezing temperatures for hours. Even some people at Mission Control thought the men were doomed.

In the end, the astronauts got the job done. Cold and hungry, they made a safe splash landing in the ocean. Talk about hanging tough. This parachute thing was a walk in the park.

"Just one more hour to go," Sally said to herself. "No sweat."

To pass the time, she memorized the names of the other 34 ascans in the Astronaut Class of 1978. Six women made it. There were Anna Fisher... Rhea Seddon, the doctor... Shannon Lucid... Judy Resnick—(everyone called her J.R.)... Kathy Sullivan, and, of course, herself, Sally Ride.

Now for the men. Steve Hawley, the redhead, was here. Who else? Sally pictured the names on the ascan roster: Bluford, Brandenstein, Buchli, Covey...no, Coats, then Covey, Creighton, Fabian, Fisher, Gardner, Gibson, Gregory, Griggs, Hart, Hauck, Hawley... Sally knew all 35 names, in order, by the time her feet hit the ground.

Sally shook her legs to get the blood circulating. Then she packed up her parachute and hoisted the heavy bag onto her back. It felt like solid lead. Parachuting was sheer

The Secret Training of the Mercury 13

In the early 1960s, the Mercury 7 astronauts were making headline history. But behind the scenes, women pilots were making secret history. These women, 25 in all, took part in a private study by a doctor and pilot named Randolph Lovelace. His goal was to find out if women were strong enough to be astronauts. They were—and then some.

The women took 75 grueling physical and mental tests. The tests were the same as or similar to the tests for male astronauts. The women had cold water squirted into their ears. They whirled around on a fast-spinning wheel and tried to not get dizzy, vomit, or pass out. They sat, sweating, in a superhot chamber as long as they could.

Thirteen women, later called the Mercury 13, passed all the tests. The first woman to pass, Jerrie Cobb, scored higher on many of the tests than anyone—male or female.

Cobb's highest score was on a test for isolation, or loneliness. The men's version of the test involved spending three hours in a quiet room. Jerrie Cobb and the other women suffered a much tougher ordeal. Cobb floated in a pool of water the same temperature as her body in a completely dark and silent room. Cobb felt, saw, heard, and smelled nothing. Cut off from the outside world like that, many people get scared or go a little crazy. Not Cobb. She floated for almost 10 hours straight. The next closest time, by another Mercury 13 pilot, was six and a half hours.

The study proved that women were qualified to be astronauts. In fact, they were more qualified than men in many ways. Women suffered fewer heart attacks. They stood up to cold, heat, pain, noise, and loneliness better. As a bonus, women were smaller. They fit into the closet-sized capsules better and needed less food and oxygen.

None of the women, including Jerrie Cobb, ever made it into space. The space program, declared NASA, was simply off-limits to women.

Why turn down the country's most qualified candidates? In 1962, the U.S. Congress held a hearing to discuss the issue. Astronaut John Glenn said, "If we could find any women that demonstrated they have better qualifications [than men], we would welcome them with open arms."

Of course, the Mercury 13 *did* demonstrate their ability. But as Glenn put it, "[To put women in space] isn't part of the current social order." Most members of Congress agreed with him. Astronaut training for all women was halted until 1978. By then, a new civil rights law stated that government agencies, including NASA, could not exclude people on the basis of gender or race.

For years, Jerrie Cobb and the other women pilots pressed NASA to send them into space. Cobb made one last push to be an astronaut in 1998. That year, at age 77, John Glenn made his second flight into space. Cobb, 10 years younger than Glenn, was turned down yet again.

FAST FORWARD

THE OTHER SPACE PIONEERS

All five of the other women in the "Class of 1978" flew into space.

Dr. Rhea (pronounced "ray") Seddon, a surgeon, flew on three shuttle missions from 1985 to 1993. She studied the effects of microgravity (weightlessness) on the human body and on animals, including 48 rats. NASA called her life science research "the most successful and efficient spacelab flown." On one mission, Seddon took a break from biology and experimented with the physics of toys in space. In the name of science, she played jacks and messed around with a Slinky while in orbit.

Dr. Anna Fisher, a medical doctor and chemist, was the first mother to fly into space. That was in 1984. She helped launch satellites, tested equipment, and conducted experiments. Her second mission was scrubbed after the *Challenger* accident. She took off a few years to raise her family and then returned to NASA in 1996. Among her jobs were helping to choose future astronauts and planning astronaut training for the International Space Station (ISS) missions.

Dr. Judy Resnik chose a career as an electrical engineer over being a classical pianist. In 1984, aboard the *Discovery* shuttle, Resnik set up a solar panel and used her skill with the robotic arm to knock dangerous icicles off the heat tiles on the shuttle's hull. Resnik's second mission, on January 28, 1986, was aboard the *Challenger*. At age 36, Resnik died with her six crewmates when the shuttle exploded shortly after lift-off. (See page 12 for details.)

Dr. Shannon Lucid, a biochemist (an expert on the chemistry of living things), flew on five shuttle missions from 1985 to 1997. In 1997, she set the U.S. record for the longest stay in space by living on the

Russian *Mir* space station for 188 days and 5 hours. Lucid was the first woman to earn the U.S. Congressional Space Medal of Honor. Russian President Boris Yeltsin awarded her the Order of Friendship Medal.

Dr. Kathy Sullivan, a geologist, in 1984 became the first woman to walk in space. Sally Ride also flew on that mission, Sally's second and last. On Sullivan's second mission, in 1990, she launched the Hubble Space Telescope and experimented with crystals. Sullivan flew one more mission, in 1992, before becoming the chief scientist of the National Oceanic and Atmospheric Administration (NOAA). Along with Sally Ride, Sullivan is honored in the International Space Hall of Fame.

The first six women chosen as astronauts from the Astronaut Class of 1978; left to right, Rhea Seddon, Anna Fisher, Judith Resnick, Shannon Lucid, Sally Ride, and Kathryn Sullivan. (UPI/Corbis-Bettmann.)

Shannon Lucid aboard the Mir *space station. (NASA / Russian Space Agency.)*

fun, Sally decided. Carrying a 40-pound parachute was not.

To increase her strength, Sally lifted weights regularly. Her toned muscles made her feel tougher, more confident.

"A sound body leads to a sound mind." She remembered that phrase—or something like it—from elementary school gym class.

Definitely true, Sally decided. Over the next few months, both her body and mind became sounder than ever.

Between survival-and-rescue exercises, Sally put in long hours in NASA's classrooms. She learned about weather, rockets, computers, geology, mechanics, electricity, photography, and more. Every evening, Sally studied manuals that explained every system on board the shuttle.

So many letter codes! Even the space shuttle itself was officially called an STS, for Space Transportation System. APU meant auxiliary power unit. EVA stood for extravehicular activity.

"Why don't they just call it a space walk?" Sally wondered aloud.

An MMU was a manned maneuvering unit. Translation: spacesuit.

Sally and John Fabian were assigned to the RMS—or remote manipulator system. Normal people called it the robotic arm. It was five stories high but only inches in diameter.

"Not exactly a candidate for muscle beach," Sally joked.

In space, the arm didn't need lots of muscle power. Even a two-ton satellite weighs zero in microgravity, or weightlessness.

Like a human arm, the RMS had a "shoulder." That was the joint attached to the space shuttle. The arm also had an "elbow" and a "wrist." Its "hand" had a fancier name.

"Leave it to NASA to turn a simple, four-letter word into 'end effector,'" Sally said.

The end effector looked more like a can than a hand. There were no fingers. But inside the can was a grapple, a round device with three cables. The cables closed around a payload, such as a satellite. Then they twisted shut to grab and hold the object.

The long, gangly arm was tough to control. It took concentration, skill, and lots of practice. There were two joysticks and dozens of dials, buttons, and switches.

Sally and John practiced on a simulator, a copy of the arm. Trainers coached the two astronauts. Later, the trainers would gleefully program malfs into the simulated arm. At first, though, John and Sally had to learn how to use the controls to make the arm move. Hand-eye coordination, this skill was called. Sally had practiced it on tennis courts and ball fields all her life.

Sally grabbed a joystick firmly in each hand. She couldn't see the whole arm directly. On a real flight, it would be outside the shuttle, mostly hidden from view. The arm had two TV cameras, one on its elbow and another on its wrist. The cameras sent images to the two black-and-white screens inside the cockpit.

Sally held out her own right arm to help picture the robot arm more clearly. She moved her whole arm up and down. That up-and-down movement was called *pitch*. On an airplane, Sally knew, pitch referred to the angle of the nose and tail. A low pitch meant the nose was pointing down and the tail was pointing up.

Sally moved the left-hand joystick up and back while looking at the video screens. The arm responded very slowly, making a whirring noise. It moved up and then down in a jerky motion.

"The real arm will move a lot smoother in space," a trainer assured Sally. "Just take it slow and easy."

Next, Sally changed the pitch at her elbow. Just her forearm and hand moved up and down. Then she flipped a JOINT switch from SHOULDER to ELBOW and moved the joystick again. It worked! The robotic arm moved up and down at the elbow.

Next, Sally held out her right arm. She moved it sideways, across her chest and then off to her right. Side-to-side motion is called *yaw*. Sally pushed the joystick left. Again, the robot arm matched her hand motion slowly and clumsily.

Sally experimented with the right-hand joystick. This control rotated the arm, causing it to whir and spin in a circle. Sally held her arm straight and tried to rotate just her wrist.

"Not a chance!" she said. She moved the joystick to one side and then the other. The robot's wrist spun in circles.

Next, Sally felt a trigger on the joystick. She squeezed it. The trigger made the grapple cables close. Of course, it "grabbed" nothing but air.

After a few weeks of practice, Sally and John were finally ready to grab a "payload." In the simulator, the payload was a big balloon in the shape of a blimplike satellite. It weighed next to nothing, so it floated, just as a real satellite would in space. It was so light, in fact, that the robot arm could send the "satellite" flying out of control with the slightest touch.

Eyes glued to the screens, Sally and John worked the controls together to set the arm in motion. The plodding,

Today, astronauts use improved robotic arms to launch and retrieve satellites in orbit. The arms are also vital tools in building the International Space Station (ISS). Sections of the station are flown into space separately and astronauts use the arm to assemble the pieces in orbit.

Astronauts James H. Newman and Jerry L. Ross work in space with the RMS arm on building the International Space Station, December 1998. (NASA.)

jerky slowness was agonizing. Sally was itching to just grab the arm and carry it over to the satellite. That, of course, was impossible from inside the shuttle.

An hour later, the arm was inches away from its target. Then it stopped dead.

"The arm shuts down when it gets confused," a trainer explained.

Sally and John still had to learn to work as a team. The robot arm didn't know what to do when their commands conflicted. The trainers reset the arm. This time, Sally and John got too close to the payload. The balloon popped.

The astronauts had just two years to master the mechanical beast.

"Okay," Sally said as they started over, "keep your eye on the bouncing robot."

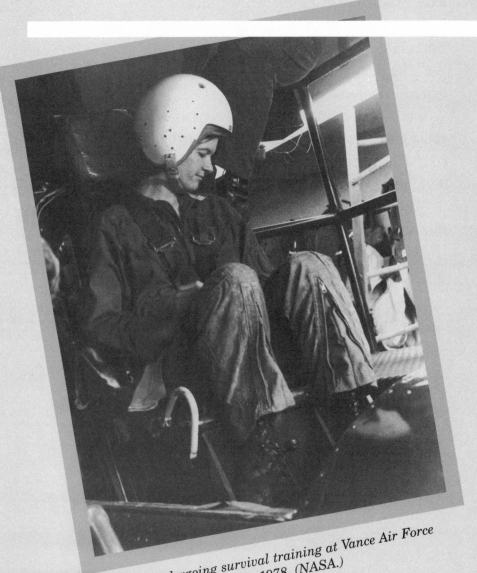

Sally Ride undergoing survival training at Vance Air Force Base, Oklahoma, August 28, 1978. (NASA.)

9

LET'S ROCK AND ROLL

"Ready for some rock and roll, Sally?" asked Brian, a trainer. Brian ran a machine that simulated spacecraft motion.

"Hey, I grew up in Los Angeles," Sally said. "I've been to Disneyland plenty of times."

Brain laughed. "Yeah, but those roller coasters only go up and down. My torture rack goes up, down, sideways, backwards, forwards—all at once."

"Can't wait," said Sally.

She meant it. Sally loved rides. They made her feel free, like flying or parachuting. Of course, NASA's "rides" weren't just fun and games, Sally knew. They trained her body to stand up to g forces, or gravity forces.

G Forces

Speeding up and slowing down both cause g forces, or gravity forces, to increase. Speeding up in your car, for example, throws you back in your seat. A sudden stop throws you forward in your seat. Here's what else g forces can do to you:

0 g   *(microgravity or zero gravity):* **Your body feels as though it doesn't weigh anything. You float in mid-air. On a roller coaster, you approach 0 g as you plummet down a steep hill. Your body starts to lift up until the coaster reaches the bottom of the hill.**

1 g   *(normal earth gravity):* **Your body feels comfortable because it is used to the pull of earth's gravity.**

Sally never noticed g forces before becoming an astronaut. Now, she thought about them every day. Just standing there, Sally was feeling 1 g: earth's gravity pulling her down. She felt a little more than 1 g each time her car sped up from 0 to 60 miles an hour. The sudden acceleration pressed her back against the seat. When the car's speed leveled out at 60, she felt normal again, back to 1 g.

Of course, the shuttle didn't zoom from 0 to 60 like a car. It zoomed from 0 to 17,000 miles per hour. Sally would feel 3 gs during lift-off. That was enough force to pin her

2 g: The face and other soft, loose parts of your body begin to droop. The body weighs twice as much as it does at 1 g, and so it presses down harder in the seat. Getting up and walking are hard to do.

3 g: Walking is impossible. You can move your arms or legs only with a lot of effort.

4 g: After a few seconds, your vision might dim. Your face becomes distorted.

5–7g: Your chest feels so heavy that you can't breathe easily. You feel tingling, cramps, dizziness, and other symptoms. After about five seconds, you might pass out.

8 g: You can't lift your arms and legs, let alone your body. You pass out within seconds.

arms and legs to the seats. Her weight would soar to 700 pounds!

Handling g forces was just like practicing a sport, Sally learned. The more you did it, the better your body got at it.

Brian worked the controls while Sally waited for her turn. She watched as Steve Hawley spun up, down, and around in the chair of the machine. His cheeks flapped and his eyes bulged. His face looked like something out of a horror movie.

Steve had warned Sally that Brian was a space history buff. He couldn't resist telling astronauts about close calls and near disasters. Right on cue, Brian said, "*Gemini 8*. March 16, 1966."

"Okay, I'll bite," Sally said. "What happened?"

"David Scott and Mr. Moonwalker himself, Neil Armstrong," Brian continued. Not that Sally could stop him now. "They were the first astronauts to dock two vehicles in orbit."

"And?" Sally couldn't help asking.

"And," Brian said, "both spacecraft joined together okay. But then they began spinning out of control, hard enough to wreck the *Gemini* capsule."

"So what happened?" Sally asked.

"Talk about g forces!" Brian said. "The astronauts practically threw up. They could hardly lift their hands to operate the controls. Armstrong tried to fire the thrusters, but that didn't work."

"What did Houston say?" asked Sally.

"Nothing. The spinning broke off voice contact with Mission Control." Brian paused for a moment to concentrate on torturing Steve.

"So what did they do?" Sally asked, finally.

"They were both about to pass out from the g forces," Brian said, "so they had no choice. Armstrong just turned off the thrusters."

"Did it work?"

Brian looked up and smiled. "Yep—just in time. The spinning stopped. But without thrusters, the mission was over. The astronauts had to come down."

"So what started the spin in the first place?" Sally

had a keen interest in knowing anything and everything that could go wrong in space.

"A thruster failed on," Brian said.

"Failed on?" asked Sally. "Like, it got stuck in the ON position?"

"Exactly. Shutting it down was the only hope. Otherwise, they both would have fried on reentry."

"Fried" was a crude word to use when talking about human beings, but Sally understood. Every astronaut thought about death. One way to lift that black cloud was to joke about it.

The machine finally stopped. Steve looked a little dizzy, but he was in one piece.

"Anyone seen my stomach?" he said, smiling.

Sally helped Steve down and then hopped into the machine and strapped herself in.

"Ready to rock and roll," she said.

Brian eased the machine into a slow, easy spin.

Sally began to hum the lullaby "Rock-a-bye, baby."

Brian laughed. "Okay, I hear you."

He adjusted the controls. The machine began to move up and down. Along with the spin, the two movements felt weird but not too bad. Then Brian really turned up the juice.

"Let the g forces be with me," Sally said, as she braced herself.

Within seconds, Sally's stomach joined Steve's— somewhere other than her body. She felt like a dizzy rag doll going through a wash cycle. The g force session left her weak-kneed. But just a few weeks ago, a ride like that would have knocked her out cold.

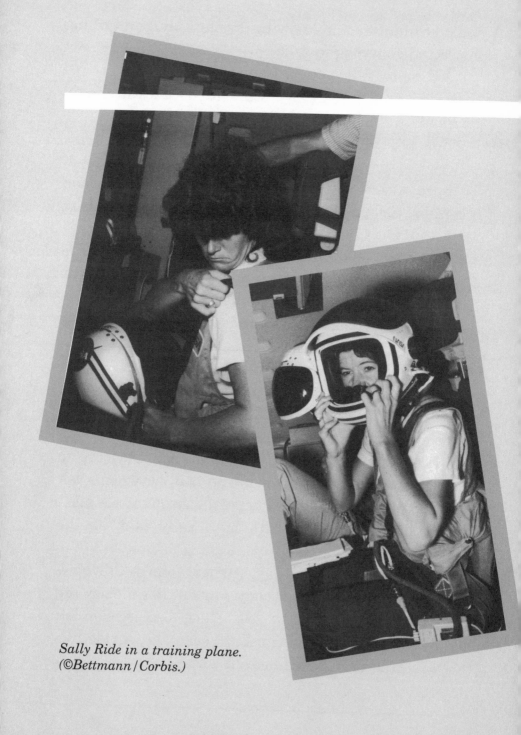

Sally Ride in a training plane.
(©Bettmann / Corbis.)

10

FLY, SALLY, FLY!

Sally felt a gentle tap on her shoulder. She turned around to see a tall, blond astronaut with a friendly face.

"Ready for a *ride*?" he asked.

Sally rolled her eyes at yet another lame pun on her last name.

"Okay, so you know my name," she said. "What's yours?"

"Hoot Gibson," the astronaut said, extending his hand.

Sally shook hands. She figured he was in another training group. That's why she hadn't met him before.

Before Sally could think of an equally bad pun on Hoot's name, the pilot spoke up: "I've got a T-38 scheduled, but my backseat driver couldn't make it. Care to join me?"

"You bet!" said Sally. The T-38 jet was her favorite part of the training. Pilots flew it for practice or to get from one NASA base to another. Mission specialists like Sally sat in

Jackie Cochran:
Pilot Superstar

Women were not allowed to be military test pilots until 1972. Some people believed that women couldn't or wouldn't fly risky aircraft. Yet that's exactly what plenty of women pilots have done, starting from the earliest days of aviation.

Jackie Cochran (1906?–1980) was one of the best. She flew high-performance planes in races and air shows from the 1930s through the 1960s. Cochran set more than 250 records for speed, altitude (height above ground), and distance. No pilot, male or female, has matched that number.

Cochran is most famous for being the first woman to break the sound barrier, or travel faster than the speed of sound. She was also one of the Mercury 13 pilots who passed astronaut training tests. (See page 60.)

In 1990, women test pilots became astronauts for the first time. (Until then, all women astronauts were mission specialists like Sally Ride.) In February 1995, an outstanding pilot named Lieutenant Colonel Eileen Collins was the first female to fly the space shuttle. In July 1999, she became the first female shuttle commander, or mission leader.

the backseat to get used to g forces and learn about high-tech aircraft.

The T-38 had a long needle for a nose and a sleek body. It looked a little like a high-tech mosquito. Sally and Hoot opened the cockpit bubble and climbed aboard.

Hoot took off smoothly and made a few fast, sharp turns and straight-up climbs. Sally knew right away he was a veteran flier. Even as the jet dove straight down toward the ground, she felt at ease.

Sally liked the T-38 so much that she made up her mind to become a pilot herself. Besides being fun, she thought it might help her chances of getting a mission. NASA loved pilots.

NASA had another training plane, the KC-135, that was nothing like the T-38. The "vomit comet," as the astronauts called it, had padded walls inside and not much else. The icky nickname was well deserved. Its roller coaster ride made most people throw up.

When their turn came, Sally, Steve, and a few others boarded the plane. They sat cross-legged on the padded floor and waited for takeoff.

Like the T-38, the vomit comet was all about g forces. In this case, though, the plane created short periods of zero gravity. Most people just called it weightlessness.

The plane climbed superhigh. Then it took a steep dive. Sally felt her body rise. She was hanging in mid-air! So was everyone and everything else inside the plane!

"Yahoooo!" she shouted. How corny! But Sally couldn't help it. The vomit comet made you feel as though you were flying.

Instant Fame or Instant Death?

Before the 1960s, no one had traveled higher than earth's atmosphere. Scientists had wild ideas about what might happen to a human in space. Would the sun's gravity crush a spaceship like a tin can? Would the ship burn to a crisp as soon as it left earth's atmosphere? Would the astronaut's blood boil or lungs explode without air pressure? No one really knew. No living creature had been in space before.

In the 19th century, no one had even flown in an airplane, let alone on a spaceship, but a few adventurers rose to dizzying heights in hot-air balloons. At just a few miles high, the temperature was as cold as the South Pole in winter. The air became too thin to breathe. "Thin air" simply meant that there was less gas in the air. Without enough oxygen, many early balloonists passed out, and a few suffocated to death. Balloonists learned to take along bottles of oxygen and to wear protective suits.

People wondered what would happen at even higher altitudes. In the 1940s and 50s, early jets carried

Sally tried to swim in the air, but she got nowhere. Then she kicked the padded wall and went zooming into the opposite wall. Luckily, that, too, was padded.

The astronauts did a few somersaults in mid-air. Sally pretended to lift Steve with a single finger.

"Don't try this at home, kids," she joked.

pilots to the top layers of the atmosphere. In a very risky experiment, Colonel Randolph Lovelace bailed out of a jet flying more than seven and a half miles high. A thick suit protected his skin from the blast of icy air. But when the parachute opened, the sudden slowdown made Lovelace pass out. Wind stripped off his gloves, causing frostbite, but Lovelace woke up and survived the landing. Lovelace later conducted the Mercury 13 astronaut training study of women pilots. (See page 60).

The next step was to find out what would happen to a living creature in space. For its first "live" flight, in 1951, the United States sent a monkey and 11 mice into space. All creatures, great and small, returned safely.

The flights proved that space travel was possible in an airtight capsule. On April 12, 1961, cosmonaut Yuri Gagarin earned instant fame as the first person to fly above earth's atmosphere.

After a few more corny yahoos, it was over. Everyone and everything dropped to the floor of the plane. Zero g only lasted as long as the plane was in free fall—about two minutes. Then the vomit comet began climbing again so that it could take another dive.

By 1979, Sally Ride and her classmates were full-fledged

astronauts. That meant they could be chosen at any time for a mission. But the training was far from over. Active astronauts still take classes and practice operating the spacecraft in sims.

Near the end of 1981, Sally was chosen as capcom, or capsule communicator, for STS-2, the second space shuttle mission. As capcom, she stayed on the ground and relayed messages to and from astronauts in space. Sally was the first woman to serve as capcom, but she was glad nobody made a big deal out of that. Unlike astronauts, capcoms were heard but not seen. They didn't usually make front-page news.

SALLY'S FUTURE

In 1984, Commander Robert Crippen chose Sally Ride to fly on a second mission with him. The crew of flight STS-41G included Jon McBride (pilot), Sally Ride (flight engineer and mission specialist), Kathy Sullivan (mission specialist), Dave Leestma (mission specialist), Marc Garneau (payload specialist), and Paul Scully-Power (payload specialist).

Ride was training for a third mission at the time the *Challenger* blew up. (See page 12.) All missions were scrubbed for several years. Ride headed a committee to plan NASA's future in space. Then she left NASA to teach and research physics at a university.

Even so, the job was an honor. Capcoms usually got chosen to fly into space on an upcoming mission. Sally tried not to get her hopes up too high.

The next month, the crew list for STS-7 was posted. Robert Crippen was the commander. With input from John Young and George Abbey, he picked his own crew. This time, he needed specialists to operate the robotic arm.

"Sally Ride," Crip told reporters, "is the best candidate for the job."

CHAPTER 11

A MARRIAGE AND A MISSION

"The hardest part of being an astronaut," Sally said to Steve Hawley, "isn't the training. It's facing the media."

Sally agreed to interviews whenever she could. Every astronaut did. That was part of the deal. But now that Sally was about to fly, reporters wanted to know every last thing about her. So did strangers. People she didn't even know wore t-shirts that said "Ride, Sally, Ride!"

There was one huge secret Sally made sure reporters and strangers didn't know. Sally and Steve had decided to get married. They both wanted a quiet ceremony—no reporters, no press conferences, no comment.

"Think we can pull it off?" Sally asked Steve.

"Let's see," Steve said. "We're the first astronauts to marry each other. You're about to be the first American woman in space. Doesn't sound like much of a news story to me."

Sally Ride being greeted by her husband, Steve Hawley, in Ellington Texas, June 24, 1983. (© Bettmann-Corbis.)

Sally laughed. It *was* a story, a huge story.

On a hot day in July 1982, Sally slipped on a pair of slacks and a rugby shirt and hopped into the cockpit of a small plane. She flew from Texas to Salina, Kansas, Steve's hometown.

There, in casual clothes, Steve and Sally got married. Bear, Sally's sister, and Steve's father, also a minister, performed the ceremony. Afterward, the couple flew off in Sally's plane for a short honeymoon.

"How was the honeymoon?" reporters asked when Sally and Steve returned. They learned about the wedding after the fact.

"Short," was all that Sally replied.

For the next 10 months, Sally's training schedule doubled. She and the crew spent hours in the simulators. They had no time to feed information to the hungry press, so the reporters grew hungrier.

Shortly before the mission in June of 1983, NASA finally scheduled a press conference. All five astronauts sat before reporters at a long table. Crip, Fred, John, Norm, and Sally each had a microphone. But almost all the questions were for Sally alone.

"Will you take lipstick or perfume into space?"

"I haven't decided," Sally replied, patiently.

"Will you wear a bra?"

Sally smiled. She couldn't believe someone actually asked that. "I don't think I'll need one," she said. "It's weightless up there, remember?"

The crew of STS-7 fields embarrasing questions from reporters. (UPI / Corbis-Bettmann.)

Changing Attitudes About Women Astronauts

The first woman in space, Valentina Tereshkova, orbited Earth in 1963. Yuri Gagarin, the first man in space, said Valentina "was born for space."

Other people of the era weren't as accepting. Al Bean, one of twelve Apollo astronauts who walked on the moon, stated that space travel was "a man's job." Spacecraft and computers were "male things," he added. Bean thought women couldn't handle the physical part.

In 1978, Bean became an astronaut trainer. After working with Sally Ride and other women astronauts, he admitted he was wrong. "Women perform the mental and physical tasks as well as males do," Bean said. After listening to a woman engineer lead a lecture at NASA, Bean said, "She knows more about heat shields than I do. It's not a male thing."

Most negative attitudes, like Bean's, changed over time. Others didn't. Before her 1983 flight, Sally Ride

"Do you plan to have children?"

Sally was stunned. *That* was none of the world's business. After a few seconds of silence, she said, "You notice I'm not answering that. Next question."

"Do you weep when something goes wrong on the job?"

The crew and some of the other reporters tensed.

"How come you don't ask Rick that question?" Sally joked. Everyone, including Rick, laughed.

looked forward to a day when "the country could just send up a woman astronaut and nobody would think twice about it."

Twenty-five years later, Eileen Collins echoed Ride's words. She was the first woman to pilot a mission and to command a mission. Like Ride, Collins didn't think being a woman was such a huge deal. She told reporters she just wanted to do her job.

Eileen Collins, STS-93 Commander, February 8, 1999. (NASA.)

Humor rarely failed. The next questions were actually about the mission. Crip even got to answer a couple. Then a reporter in the front row looked directly at Sally: "How does it feel to be the first American woman chosen for a mission?"

Sally replied, "I did not come to NASA to make history. It's important to me that people don't think I was picked for the flight because I am a woman, and it's time for NASA to send one."

Crip chimed in, "I picked Sally for this mission because she's an expert at the robotic arm, and we need that expertise on this mission."

Case closed.

"Do you feel like a hero?" a reporter in the back shouted.

Sally sighed. NASA could have picked Judy Resnik, Rhea Seddon, Shannon Lucid, Anna Fisher, or Kathy Sullivan for this mission. They just happened to pick Sally first. No, she didn't feel like a hero, but she knew a lot of people would look at her that way.

Sally finally answered, "When I was an 11-year-old girl, there weren't any women astronauts. When I fly, girls will see that there's a place for them in the space program. If that makes me a hero, then I guess I'm a hero."

12

RIDE, SALLY RIDE

Sally sure didn't feel like a hero. After nearly four hours flat on her back, she ached all over. She wore a parachute, a folded life raft, boots, gloves, a helmet, and a flight suit. All that gear almost doubled her weight.

Worse, Sally had to go to the bathroom. Because of the long wait between boarding and launch, astronauts wore diapers during lift-off. Diapers! There was no choice. They couldn't just get up and go to the bathroom in the middle of a launch.

The only thing worse than wearing a diaper was wearing a wet diaper, Sally decided. She glanced at the Mission Time Clock. T minus 5 minutes 22 seconds and counting. She'd make it. In less than an hour the shuttle would be in orbit. Then she could use the toilet.

Sally soon forgot all about diapers, wet or otherwise. The final countdown began at T minus 5 minutes.

"*Challenger*, start the APUs," said a voice over the astronauts' headsets.

"Roger," replied Crip, who was sitting in front of Sally. "Start the APUs."

Rick, the pilot, flipped a switch to turn on the APUs, the auxiliary power units. These motors steered the rocket engines. The cockpit shook gently.

Sally's stomach began to churn. It wasn't nerves. She was just plain scared—and happy. Was that possible?

Buttons and computer displays on the instrument panels lit up and alarms sounded and stopped. Needles on the gauges flickered.

"Normal system checks," Sally reminded herself. "Just like in the simulator."

T minus 2 minutes.

"*Challenger*, close visors."

Sally flipped down the visor on her helmet. The helmet filled with cool, refreshing oxygen.

T minus 1 minute 57 seconds.

"*Challenger*, H-two tank pressurization okay. You are go for launch, over."

"Roger," confirmed Crip. "Go for launch, out."

The mighty hydrogen fuel tanks were building up pressure.

Sally felt the cockpit shake, rumble, and sway back and forth.

"Just a steering check," she reminded herself.

T minus 25 seconds.

The motors for the solid rocket boosters switched on. The space shuttle's computers took over the launch.

"My life is in the hands of machines," Sally thought. Then she smiled. "Do machines have hands?"

T minus 10 seconds.

"Go for main engine start," said a voice over Sally's headset.

"Six... five... four..."

The three liquid-fuel engines roared to life. The shaking was so rough, Sally felt as though she were in a blender. The noise hurt her ears.

"two, one..."

The solid rocket boosters fired. There was no stopping now. Once the solid rockets lit, they stayed lit.

"Lift-off!"

Sally was thrown back into her seat. The noise was deafening. She felt helpless, overwhelmed.

"Something's wrong," she thought. "It's way too rough."

The lift-off was nothing at all like the simulator! No amount of training could prepare a person for this kind of ride.

"Roll program!" Crip shouted.

Sally relaxed a bit. She could hear Crip's voice over the headset in her helmet. Roll program meant that the shuttle was turning to the right to aim for the ocean. All systems go.

Somehow, the shaking, rumbling, and roaring increased. Sally's head felt like a ping pong ball rattling around in the helmet.

"How does this thing hold together?" she thought. She worried that parts had shaken loose or broken apart, but the warning lights were clear.

"Throttle up!" Sally heard Crip say.

As the engines revved to full power, the g forces increased. Sally felt her cheeks being stretched and twisted. Her body felt like lead.

She strained her neck to look out the window. In just seconds, they were above the clouds. The sky was changing from blue to pitch black.

"Stars!" she said aloud.

A sudden bang rattled Sally's bones. Fire covered the window! The shuttle was inside a ball of white-orange flame!

"Control, we have SRB separation," said Crip.

SRB stands for solid rocket booster. The rockets had burned up all their fuel and separated from the shuttle. The fireball outside the window disappeared. So did the shaking and the roaring. The cockpit fell eerily silent. There wasn't enough air outside to carry sound vibrations.

"*Challenger*, you are negative return. Do you copy? Over."

"Roger, Control," Crip replied. "Negative return, out."

There was no turning back. The shuttle was going too fast and had flown too far to go back to Cape Canaveral. If they had to abort, they would have to make an emergency landing. With luck, the shuttle could reach Europe or Africa.

"Or Hawaii," Sally thought, remembering last week's crash simulation.

Then came good news. "Control," said Crip, "we are single-engine press to MECO, over."

MECO was Main Engine Cut-Off. Single-engine press meant that if two engines failed, the last one could still get the shuttle into orbit. Sally forgot about emergency landings and concentrated on checking the instruments for malfs and nits.

Just minutes after sitting on the launchpad, the shuttle was traveling 20 times faster than sound. It slowly flattened out and rolled so that it was flying upside down. Earth appeared out the window, or at least part of it did. The shuttle flew too close to it for the astronauts to see the whole planet.

The engines throttled up for a last, big push into orbit. Sally braced herself for the strongest g forces of the flight. She felt as if a sofa pinned down her whole body. Thanks to g-force training, the feeling was familiar. But it didn't seem to stop. Sally tried to lift her head to read the instruments. No go.

After two minutes of feeling like a squashed bug, Sally couldn't wait to get into orbit. Then, moments later, Sally's arms lifted off the seat without effort. She was weightless! Pencils and checklists floated in the air. Sally grabbed them and stuck them to patches of Velcro on the wall.

"OMS two cut-off," said Crip, switching off the shuttle's last engine.

The space shuttle was in orbit! They were traveling 25 times faster than sound, five miles every second. Yet Sally couldn't even tell they were moving.

Sally Ride communicating with ground controllers from mid-deck of the earth-orbiting space shuttle Challenger. *(© Bettmann-Corbis.)*

A new voice came over her headset. "What's it like up there, Sally?" said the capcom.

What was it *like*? A shuttle flight was like nothing on earth. Then Sally smiled. "Ever been to Disneyland? This is better than an E ticket!"

An E ticket was a pass to all of Disneyland's best rides. Sally was on the best ride in the world.

Ride, Sally Ride!

13

SOARING INTO HISTORY

Sally let go of a cookie in the galley, or kitchen. It just hung there in mid-air. She floated over to it, mouth open, and took a bite. It wasn't easy. Her first push-off had been too hard. She flew past the cookie into the opposite wall.

"My turn," said John Fabian. He made the cookie spin like a top and then ate it, no hands.

The cookie-eating game quickly turned into a contest. Astronauts couldn't resist a little friendly competition.

Once the cookies were gone, the astronauts took turns tossing peanuts and jelly beans into each others' mouths. The jelly beans were a gift from President Ronald Reagan.

"We need something to wash these down," Sally said, pouring orange juice in the air. Instead of falling, the juice formed a perfect orange sphere. It floated like the cookies and jelly beans. John and Sally took turns dipping a straw into the ball and drinking the juice.

Sally laughed. Here they were, two highly trained astronauts, playing with food! She couldn't help it. Being weightless was strange and wonderful. Sally felt constantly off-balance. The push of a finger off a wall sent her tumbling in a slow somersault. She learned to grab rungs and straps to stop her body.

Sally's body felt strange, too. Her dark hair was floating all around her head. On earth, gravity pulled her body fluids down, toward her feet. In space, the fluids spread all over her body, making her legs skinnier and her face and chest puffier.

Every 90 minutes, the shuttle circled the earth. Sally saw 16 sunsets and 16 sunrises that day, and each day, in space. The stars, Sally noticed, never looked clearer or brighter.

Sally photographed the blue and white earth below. "I feel like a tourist," she said, as she clicked another picture, "a camera in every pocket."

Earth curved and ended abruptly at the inky black space. The atmosphere looked like a paper-thin film just above the planet surface. Sally could see clouds, oceans, and land clearly. The more she looked, the more she saw. Electrical storms flashed in the clouds. A white, swirling hurricane was forming over the Atlantic Ocean. At one glance, Sally saw coast to coast across the United States. Houston, Texas, looked like a tiny, detailed map. Sally could even pick out the launchpad at Cape Canaveral, Florida.

Sightseeing and microgravity games were only a brief relief from the tight schedule of tasks. Sally and John conducted dozens of experiments. One involved a colony of ants. Students in Camden, New Jersey, set it up. A TV camera recorded how the little insects moved in microgravity.

"Just like us," Sally predicted. "A little clumsy and off-balance at first, but you get used to it. Heck, you get to love it."

College students wanted to see if radish seeds sprouted roots up, down, or every which way in space. Companies wanted to grow perfect crystals in microgravity for scientists to study.

Each day, Norm monitored all the astronauts for changes in their bodies due to microgravity. Muscles weakened, and bones lost calcium since they didn't have to work as hard.

The astronauts had to exercise on treadmills to stay strong. No one liked to do it. Sweat clung to the body, instead of running off or evaporating. After the first treadmill session, Sally felt a wet pool stuck to the small of her back.

That night, Sally tried to calm down in order to sleep. She listened to music on her headphones and drifted off. Then she woke up, feeling weird. Her arms and legs floated in front of her. Her head bobbed in rhythm with her neck pulse. Sally crawled into a sleeping bag and zipped herself in to keep her limbs in place.

"Night, John Boy," she said, echoing the hit TV program *The Waltons.*

"Night, Sally," replied John.

"Night, John," added Norm.

The joke went full circle around the crew, and then Sally said, "Good night, Houston."

"Showtime," Sally said to John the next morning.

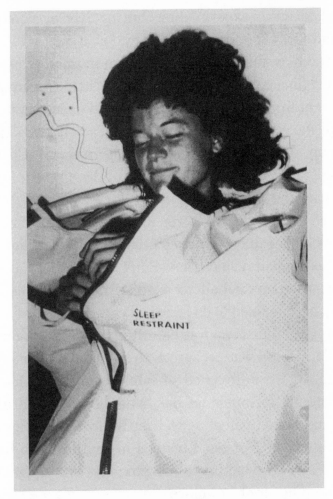

Sally Ride in her sleeping bag aboard Challenger.
(© Bettmann-Corbis.)

"Let's do it," John replied.

Sally and John floated over to the robotic arm controls and strapped their feet to the wall. Using the robotic arm was the most important part of the mission.

The first challenge was a warm-up. The two astronauts

worked as a team to unbend the long arm and move it toward a satellite stored in the cargo bay. Then Sally very slowly gripped the satellite and lifted it into space. She pressed a trigger. The satellite floated freely against a black backdrop.

At Sally's command, Crip fired a thruster. The gas jet caused the satellite to spin.

"Wow!" Sally said. "That spin's a lot faster than we thought."

She grasped the satellite with the arm. She didn't want it to spin out of reach.

Sally and John practiced holding, releasing, and spinning the satellite over and over. They had to perfect the procedure so that future crews could repair and release satellites without mishap.

"Getting hot," Sally said, as she looked at the temperature gauge for the satellite. Overheating could burn out the satellite's systems.

"Power down the satellite," Sally ordered. "That'll cool things down a little."

"What else can we do?" John asked.

Sally came up with a great idea. "Let's move the shuttle so the satellite is in its shadow," she said. "Without sunlight, the temperature will drop big-time."

John and Sally ran the idea by Crip.

"It'll be tricky," Crip said. "If the satellite hits the heat tiles, it could do some real damage."

Without heat tiles, the astronauts would burn up during reentry.

"Let's do it," Crip said to Rick.

The pilots fired thrusters in short bursts while John and Sally watched the instruments.

When the tricky maneuver was over, Sally checked the temperature gauges. The satellite cooled down quickly. She looked at one of the RMS videos. The robotic arm's camera showed a white, mothlike space shuttle against black space. It was the first time such a picture had been taken.

"Beautiful!" shouted Rick at the sight. To Mission Control, he reported, "You've got five happy people here."

"Roger, *Challenger*," said the capcom. "There are several thousand happy people down here."

Sally and John played satellite toss-and-fetch several more times during the mission. Most tests worked well. But then a malf popped up.

Sally said, "I extended the end effector and got no joy." The hand was stuck!

"Frozen?" John suggested.

"Maybe," Sally said. She tried moving it a few more times. "Definitely," she said.

Losing a satellite in space wasn't an option. But Sally knew what to do. Very slowly and gently, she tapped the robot arm against the cargo door. It worked. The gentle jolt was just enough to loosen the end effector without damaging the shuttle.

"Ready to retrieve," Sally said.

The arm inched back over to the satellite, and the can-like hand swallowed a part that was sticking out. Sally pulled the trigger to close the grapple cables.

"Got it!" she said. Both she and John let out a sigh of relief. "Perfect," Sally thought, "no mistakes."

Sally slowly set the satellite back in the cargo bay and closed the doors.

"Mission accomplished," John said.

After six short, busy days in orbit, the space shuttle was ready to land.

"Too much weather in Florida," Crip reported to the crew. "California, here we come."

Sally's first thought was that her family would be disappointed. They were waiting for her in Florida. Her second thought was that the landing strip at Edwards Air Force Base in California was much shorter than the shuttle's usual runway.

"It beats Honolulu, though," thought Sally.

Less than an hour later, the shuttle had traveled halfway around the world. It had dropped 200 miles out of the sky. Its back wheels touched down on the hard pavement gently, almost too soft to feel. The shuttle zoomed down the runway at 200 miles an hour. The nose and the cockpit slowly descended. The nose wheels landed with a thump, and the space shuttle braked to a stop.

All five astronauts clapped and cheered.

Adjusting to earth's gravity took a while. As Sally rose from her seat, the whole room spun. Her brain still expected her to float, so Sally felt very heavy. Her arms and legs took a lot of effort to lift. She could stand, but she couldn't walk in a straight line. She and the crew did exercises to get used to their bodies again. A doctor checked them out and

Sally Ride walking away from the space shuttle Challenger *upon landing, followed by astronauts John Fabian and Frederick Hauck. (© Bettmann-Corbis.)*

gave a thumbs-up. Then, after half an hour, they all finally had their "earth legs."

The hatch opened. Crip stepped out first. He smiled broadly and squinted his eyes in the bright sunshine.

Sally was next. She put one foot out of the hatch and onto the top step of a tall stairway. It was one giant leap for humans, men and women.

Sally Kristen Ride grinned and waved as she stepped out of the space shuttle and into the history books.

CONTINUING SALLY RIDE'S MISSION: YOUR FUTURE IN SPACE

Sally Ride was 32 years old when she went on her pioneering mission. What will space exploration be like when you're 32? The mid-21st century might seem like a long way off, but experts are already planning for our future in space. As head of a NASA planning group in the 1980s, Sally Ride and her team proposed four goals for the future of space travel.

Goal 1: Mission Earth: Study and improve our planet from earth orbit.

Consider it mission accomplished—and ongoing. The first step was to deploy hundreds of satellites. Our eyes in the sky now spot shrinking rain forests, track hurricanes, help scientists predict which volcanos are about to erupt, locate the ruins of past civilizations, and more.

A next step for Mission Earth is the International Space Station (ISS). The ISS is an orbiting science lab and a space factory for making products such as crystals, which turn out better in microgravity. To staff the ISS, NASA needs scientists, engineers, mechanics, doctors, and other skilled people. These people spend months, instead of days or weeks, working in orbit. Would you want to be one of them?

Goal 2: Explore the solar system.

Space probes (pilotless spacecraft) don't need food, air, water, or artificial gravity to explore space. Also, if one crashes or gets lost, we can replace it. For those reasons, space probes can travel farther and faster in space than humans can. Plus, they can do it for a much lower cost. Why should space probes visit Mars, Jupiter, Saturn, asteroids, comets, and other solar system wonders?

"To explain the unexplained," said Sally Ride. "Anything new and interesting that we can learn opens our eyes and ears. It's our traditional nature, our natural curiosity to explore the unknown."

Behind every space probe is a large team of humans on the ground. The team includes computer programmers, scientists, engineers, technicians, space artists, and others.

Goals 3 and 4: Explore and colonize the moon and Mars.

Space probes are locating sources of water and other usable resources on Mars and the moon. Their findings could eventually lead to permanent human colonies.

Sally Ride predicted, "The 10-year-olds of today will be involved in human missions to Mars. They will be going there, on the ground planning and supporting missions, learning about the history of Mars, investigating life on Mars, and doing science experiments. Engineers will be building and planning things to get us there. Teachers will teach about [human missions to Mars] in school."

Why risk sending humans into space? Why not just send space probes?

"It's the same reason geologists go to Tibet or scientists go to Antarctica," explained Ride. "Humans can react to anything new and follow a new line of investigation. They can think about it and decide what to do. There are things that machines do better than humans, but people need to be in space."

Besides scientists and engineers, future colonies will need all the people who make your community work: teachers, writers, artists, political leaders, business people, office workers, entertainers, and so on.

Are you up to the challenge?

"Reach for the stars!" is Sally Ride's advice.

TIMELINES

The World During Sally Ride's Life

1957   Launch of *Sputnik*, the first human-made object to orbit earth.

1958   Formation of the National Aeronautics and Space Administration (NASA).

1960   Proclamation by President John F. Kennedy that an American would walk on the moon by the end of the decade.

1961   Flight of Yuri Gagarin, the first human in space.

1962   Flight of John Glenn, the first American to orbit earth.

1963   Flight of Valentina Tereshkova, the first woman in space; assassination of President Kennedy.

1964   The Vietnam War began.

1968   Assassinations of Martin Luther King, Jr. and Robert Kennedy.

1969   First moon landing, by Neil Armstrong and Buzz Aldrin.

1974   Resignation of President Richard Nixon due to the Watergate break-in scandal.

1975   U.S. and Soviet Union docked (linked) spacecraft in orbit during the Apollo-Soyuz mission. The Vietnam War ended.

1981   Orbit of the first piloted space shuttle, *Columbia*.

1983   Flight of Sally Ride, the first American woman in space.

1986   *Challenger* space shuttle accident.

1990   Union of East and West Germany into one nation.

1991   The Persian Gulf War; break-up of the Soviet Union into Russia, Ukraine, Latvia, and other independent countries.

1992   Flight of Mae Jemison, the first African-American woman in space.

1995   Flight of Eileen Collins, the first woman to pilot a space shuttle.

1996   Shannon Lucid's stay on *Mir* space station, the longest time in space for an American astronaut (233 days).

1999   Construction of the International Space Station (ISS); flight of Eileen Collins, the first woman to command a shuttle mission.

Sally Ride's Life

1951   Birth of Sally Kristen Ride on May 26 in Encino, California, a suburb of Los Angeles.

1968   High school graduation from the Westlake School for Girls in Los Angeles.

1973   Bachelor degrees in physics and English from Stanford University in Palo Alto, California.

1975   Master's degree in physics from Stanford.

1977   NASA allows women to join the Astronaut Corps for the first time.

1978   Ph.D. degree in physics from Stanford; astronaut training.

1982   Marriage to astronaut Steven Hawley.

1983   At age 32, Ride becomes the youngest astronaut and the first American woman in space.

1984   Ride's second space shuttle mission.

1986   *Challenger* explosion and accident investigation.

1987   Panel, headed by Ride, to plan NASA's future in space; divorce from Hawley; physics teaching post at Stanford University.

1989   Teaching post at the University of California in San Diego (U.C.S.D.); director of the California Space Institute (C.S.I.).

2000   In addition to teaching at U.C.S.D., Sally Ride continues to give speeches to students and others about space exploration.

GLOSSARY OF SPACE WORDS

Astronaut candidate (or "ascan"): An astronaut-to-be who has begun training.

Avionics: Electrical systems that control the flight of an aircraft or spacecraft.

Capsule communicator (or "capcom"): The person at Mission Control who relays messages to and from astronauts in space.

Cockpit: The section of an aircraft or space vehicle where the pilot and flight crew sit.

Cosmonaut: Russian term for *astronaut*.

Flight simulation (or "sim"): A computer program that copies the conditions and situations of a flight in a simulator. The shuttle's simulators are copies of the cockpit that never leave the ground.

Fuel cell: A device that combines hydrogen and oxygen into water and electricity.

G force: A unit that measures the force exerted on a body due to gravity or acceleration (speeding up and slowing down).

Malfunction (or "malf"): Serious problem with a spacecraft system.

Nit: Minor problem with a spacecraft system.

Orbital Maneuvering System (OMS): A space shuttle engine.

Remote Manipulator System (RMS): The shuttle's robotic arm.

Space Transportation System (STS): The space shuttle and its fuel tanks and rockets.

Thruster: A gas jet that, when fired, changes the speed or direction of a spacecraft.

RESOURCES

Bibliography:

Buchanan, Doug. *Air & Space* (Female Firsts in Their Fields). Chelsea House, 1999.

Briggs, Carole S.*Women in Space* (A&E Biographies). Lerner, 1998.

Maze, Stephanie. *I Want to Be an Astronaut*. Harcourt Brace, 1999.

Mullane, Mike. *Liftoff! An American Dream*. Silver Burdett, 1995.

Ride, Sally with Susan Okie. *To Space and Back*. Beech Tree, 1986.

Ride, Sally and Tam O'Shaughnessy. *The Third Planet: Exploring the Earth from Space*, Crown, 1994.

———. *The Mystery of Mars*. Crown, 1999.

The Space Shuttle Operator's Manual. Beacontree Press, 1988.

Web sites and addresses:

Kids Discover magazine ("Astronauts," "Solar System," "Space," and other related issues): 149 Fifth Av., New York, NY 10010.

Mars 2020: A Space Exploration Game: Aristoplay, 450 S. Wagner Rd., Ann Arbor, MI 48103; www.aristoplay.com

NASA—Johnson Space Center:
http://www.jsc.nasa.gov/pac/students

NASA—"How to Become an Astronaut":
http://www.observe.ivv.nasa.gov/spacefly/howto.html

Odyssey magazine: Cobblestone Publishing, 30 Grove St.,
Peterborough, NH 03458;
www.odysseymagazine.com

U.S. Astronaut Hall of Fame: 6225 Vectorspace Blvd.,
Titusville, FL 32780;
www.astronauts.org

U.S. Space Camp: P.O. Box 070015, Huntsville, AL 35807;
www.spacecamp.com

Women in Aviation Resource Center (including the Mercury 13):
www.aircruise.com/wia/

Women Astronauts: userpages.aug.com/captbarb/astronauts

Young Astronaut Council: 1308 19th St NW, Washington D.C.
20036;
www.yac.org

INDEX

Note: Page numbers in italics refer to photographs.